English for
Construction

2

Vocational English
Course Book

Evan Frendo

Series editor David Bonamy

Contents

1 Teamwork

- talk about roles and responsibilities
- explain how an organisation works
- describe your job and experience
- write your CV
- discuss roles in an international construction project

Roles and responsibilities

Speaking **1** Look at this illustration. Say what the people's jobs are and what they do.

Vocabulary **2** Match these descriptions with the people in the illustration in 1.

1 I'm a driver. I work for a concrete supplier. We deliver concrete to construction sites all over the country. ☐
2 I'm a master electrician. This is my apprentice. ☐ ☐
3 I'm a painter. Today I'm painting a steel staircase. ☐
4 I'm a security guard. I control access to the site. I'm responsible to the site manager. ☐
5 I'm the site manager. My company is responsible for the whole project. ☐
6 We're reporters. We're visiting the site to ask some questions. ☐

3 Name as many items in the illustration in 1 as you can. Compare your list with a partner.

ladder, …

Speaking　**4**　Work in pairs. Either a) Explain what your job is and what you do. Or b) Imagine you work on the construction site in 1. Explain what your job is and what you do.

I'm a … I work for … My company … I'm responsible for …

Listening　**5**　▶ 🎧 02　Two reporters are visiting Martin Karp from Karp Construction. Listen to their conversation. What do the reporters want?

6　Listen again and complete these sentences.

1　Karp Construction is the _____ .
2　Martin Karp is the _____ .
3　Sabina Tom is the _____ .
4　Kasper Karp owns _____ .
5　Mr Lang represents the _____ .
6　Anna Black works for the _____ .
7　Robert Lane is _____ .

Language

Present simple and present continuous	
We use the **present simple** to talk about routines and things that are permanent or happen all the time.	*I **control** access to the site.* *She **works for** the cement supplier.*
We use the **present continuous** to talk about things that take place at the time of speaking and are not permanent.	*We'**re visiting** the site.* *He'**s walking** through the gate.*
We use **adverbs of frequency** (e.g. *always, usually, often, sometimes, never*) with the present simple to describe how often somebody does something or how often something happens.	*We **usually** have about 100 people on site.* ***Sometimes** we work in a consortium.*

7　Martin's assistant is giving more information about people's roles on site. Choose the correct verb forms to complete this text.

' … So, as Martin said, we (1) *have / are having* around 100 people on site every day. Today, most people (2) *work / are working* on the basic structure of the building. The people in green jackets over there are concrete finishers from DKI Cement, the cement supplier. On this project, they (3) *supervise / are supervising* the unskilled labourers, who are all local people. Of course, there are always a lot of heavy equipment operators. They (4) *handle / are handling* the cranes, the cement mixers, the cement pumps, and so on. The drivers (5) *bring / are bringing* in fresh loads of cement several times a day. Over there, a couple of painters (6) *paint / are painting* the staircase, and the electricians (7) *repair / are repairing* one of the generators.'

Speaking　**8**　Work in small groups to discuss these questions.

1　What's the difference between a general contractor and a subcontractor?
2　What's a consortium?
3　What suppliers are typical on a construction site?
4　In audio script 2 on page 70, Martin Karp says, 'We **co-ordinate all the subcontractors** and make sure things **stay on schedule** and **stay within budget**.' What do the expressions in bold mean?

Structure of an organisation

Vocabulary **1** Look at this organisation chart of a construction company. Then complete the sentences with the words in the box.

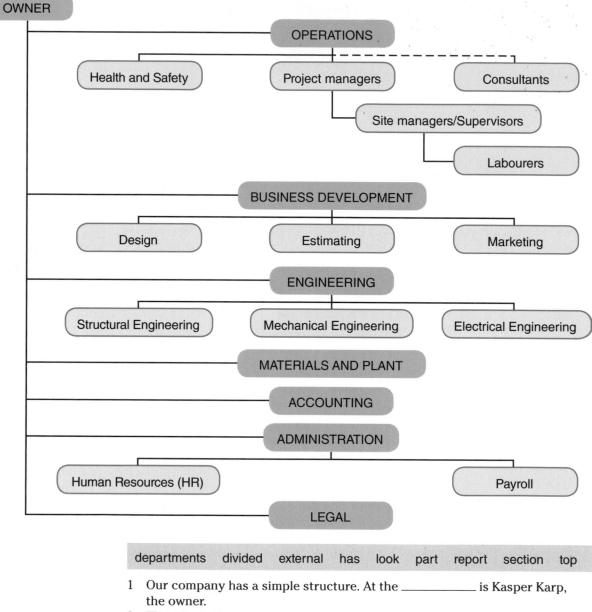

OWNER

OPERATIONS

Health and Safety | Project managers | Consultants

Site managers/Supervisors

Labourers

BUSINESS DEVELOPMENT

Design | Estimating | Marketing

ENGINEERING

Structural Engineering | Mechanical Engineering | Electrical Engineering

MATERIALS AND PLANT

ACCOUNTING

ADMINISTRATION

Human Resources (HR) | Payroll

LEGAL

| departments | divided | external | has | look | part | report | section | top |

1 Our company has a simple structure. At the _____ is Kasper Karp, the owner.
2 There are seven _____ . The department heads report to the owner.
3 Operations consists of a Health and Safety _____ and all the project managers.
4 The site managers and supervisors _____ directly to a project manager.
5 Business Development is _____ into three sections: Design, Estimating and Marketing.
6 Engineering also _____ three sections: Structural, Mechanical and Electrical.
7 There are different departments which _____ after materials and plant, accounting, administration and legal.
8 Sometimes we have _____ consultants to help with special jobs. They are not _____ of the company.

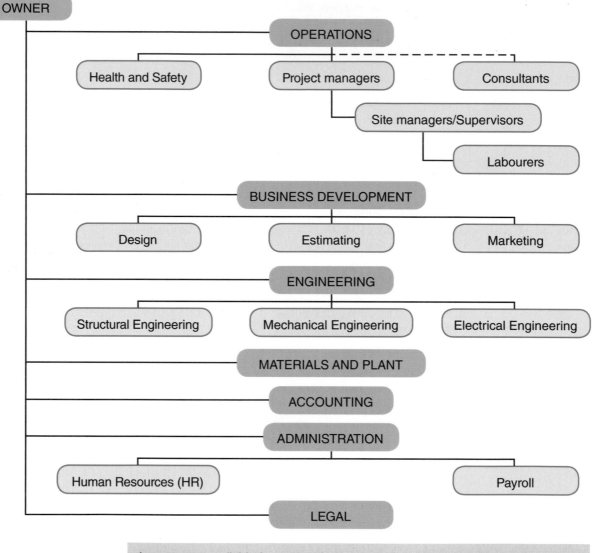

2 ▶ ⚡ **03** Listen to the heads of the seven departments talking about their roles. Write the names of their departments. Use the organisation chart in 1 to help you.

1 _____
2 _____
3 _____
4 _____
5 _____
6 _____
7 _____

3 Listen again. Write the expressions used to talk about roles and responsibilities.

1 *make sure*, _____
2 _____
3 _____ , _____
4 _____ , _____ , *work out*, _____
5 _____ , *send out*
6 _____ , _____ , *work with*
7 _____ , _____ , _____

4 Match the sets of collocations.

1	make	a)	of
2	look	b)	sure
3	consist	c)	to
4	report	d)	after
5	liaise	e)	into
6	be responsible	f)	with
7	deal	g)	for
8	divide	h)	with

5 Complete the sentences. Use the organisation chart in 1 to help you. Sometimes more than one answer is possible.

1 The Administration department consists _____ .
2 The head of accounting reports _____ .
3 Engineering is divided _____ .
4 The project managers liaise _____ .
5 Business Development is responsible _____ .
6 The site managers make _____ .
7 There are three sections in _____ and _____ .

6 Work in pairs. Draw an organisation chart for a construction company (real or imaginary). Explain your chart to another pair.

At the top is …
This department consists of …
These people report to …

Jobs and experience

1 ▶ 🎧 04 Listen to three conversations. Match the job in each conversation with a word from the box.

using a total station

| civil engineer | concrete finisher | land surveyor |

1 _____ 2 _____ 3 _____

2 Read the questions. For each conversation, answer *yes* (Y), *no* (N), or *doesn't say* (X). Then listen again and check your answers.

	Conversation 1	Conversation 2	Conversation 3
1 Is he a manual worker?			
2 Does he work mostly indoors?			
3 Was he good at maths at school?			
4 Does he work with CAD programs?			
5 Does he use high-tech equipment on site?			
6 Did he start as an apprentice?			
7 Is he self-employed?			

Speaking **3** Work in pairs. Read the questions in the table again. Take turns to ask and answer them so that they are true for you.

A: **Are you** a manual worker?
B: No, I'm not. I'm a project manager.
A: **Do you work** mostly indoors?
B: Yes, I do. I work in an office. I'm responsible for a hospital car park project.

Language

Questions	
Questions with **be** begin with the correct form of the verb **be**, or use a rising tone.	**Are** you self-employed? **You're** self-employed? **Is** he on site today? **He's** on site today?
Questions with **do/does/did**	**Do** you work indoors? **Does** he work indoors? **Did** you go to university?
Question words (*what, where, who, how*)	**What** do you do? **Where** are they from? **Who** is the client? **How** does it work?

Speaking **4** Work in pairs. Think of a job but don't tell your partner. Take turns to ask and answer questions to find out the jobs.

Is the job indoors or outdoors?
Do you work alone or with other people?
What qualifications do you need?
What training did you do?

Reading 5 Read this CV and answer the questions about Arnold Keller.

1 How old is he?
2 Which school did he go to?
3 Where did he do his apprenticeship?
4 What is his highest qualification?
5 Does he know anything about project management?

---

*euro**pass***

Europass Curriculum Vitae

Personal information

First name(s) / Surname(s)	Arnold Keller
Address(es)	Mozartstrasse 23, Blendorf
Telephone(s)	Home: 01756 78634 Mobile: 077434 675332
Fax(es)	
E-mail	arnold@keller.de
Nationality	German
Date of birth	21.03.84
Gender	Male

Work experience

Dates	2003	2004–2007
Occupation or position held	Apprentice	Student trainee
Main activities and responsibilities	On-the-job-training	Project assistant – Motorway lay-by 2004, Bridge renovation 2005, Motorway tunnel 2006
Name and address of employer	DM Construction	DM Construction
Type of business or sector	Construction	Construction

Education and training

Dates	June 2003	June 2007
Title of qualification awarded	School Leaving Certificate	Bachelor's degree in Construction Engineering
Principal subjects/occupational skills covered	Maths, Physics, English	Health and Safety, Site management, Project management, Cost estimating
Name and type of organisation providing education and training	Blendorf Grammar School, Blendorf, Germany	Vocational College, Blendorf, Germany

Personal skills and competences

Mother tongue(s)	German
Other language(s)	English, French

Writing 6 Write your own CV. Use the Europass CV structure to help you plan and organise your details. Then swap CVs with a partner. Check that your partner's CV is clear and easy to understand.

Focus on a project: International Finance Centre (IFC) Seoul, Korea

Reading **1** Read these extracts about a new development in Seoul, Korea. What is the project?

1 Siemens-Shinwha has been awarded a contract to supply a fire safety system for the new IFC Seoul project which was developed by AIG real estate.

2 Designed by the award-winning architectural firm Arquitectonica, IFC Seoul is the leading business destination in Seoul with approximately 500,000 square metres of development.

3 The IFC Seoul is a joint venture between the Seoul Metropolitan Government and AIG Global Real Estate.

4 Established in 1968, POSCO is South Korea's largest steel producer.

5 A consortium led by GS Construction and POSCO won the contract to excavate the site. The contract for the next phase of construction was signed with a new consortium, including Daelim, POSCO, Hyundai Development and headed by GS Construction in January of this year.

6 To the south will be the 29-storey Two IFC office tower, which will offer some 79,000 square metres of floor space; to the west will be the 32-storey One IFC with 88,000 square metres, while the northern corner will be reserved for a 450-guestroom, 38-storey five-star hotel. The structure on the north-eastern side of the project, Three IFC, will be 55 storeys in height and, with a total office space of 160,000 square metres, will be the largest structure in the complex.

7 Otis Elevator Company was awarded a contract from AIG Korean Real Estate Development YH to provide 125 elevators, escalators and moving walkways for International Finance Centre (IFC) Seoul in Korea.

2 Match the organisations involved in the project with their roles. Sometimes more than one answer is possible.

1 GS Construction
2 Siemens-Shinwha
3 POSCO
4 Seoul Metropolitan Government and AIG Global Real Estate
5 Arquitectonica
6 Daelim
7 Otis Elevator Company

a) architects
b) excavation
c) fire safety equipment supplier
d) elevator manufacturer
e) owners/developers
f) consortium member
g) steel producer

Speaking **3** Work in small groups. Think of a large construction project in your area. Discuss which companies were involved and the role(s) they played.

Review

Vocabulary **1** Match 1–5 with their meanings a–e.

1 a contractor
2 an owner
3 a client
4 a consortium
5 a consultant

a) an adviser
b) a group of people or companies who work together on a project
c) a person who holds the legal rights to something
d) a customer
e) a person or company who agrees to provide materials or services for a specific price

2 Complete this description of the organisation of a company with appropriate words.

> The Berlin branch has three departments. The project management department consists (1) _____ seven sections. Each section looks (2) _____ a different project. The legal and finance department deals (3) _____ all accounting issues, as well as contracts and claims. The logistics department is responsible (4) _____ making sure that the project management department has the resources to do the job. This includes all personnel and plant. The head of the Berlin branch reports directly (5) _____ the owner, who is based in Frankfurt.

Language **3** Each of these questions has one error. Correct the errors.

1 Does you work outdoors?
2 Is you self-employed?
3 Did you done an apprenticeship?
4 Was you good at maths at school?
5 What did you doing yesterday?
6 When did you started excavating?
7 Where is supplying the elevators?

Writing **4** Write a short covering letter to a potential employer to accompany your CV. Include:

1 an introduction: introduce yourself and say where you saw the job advert.
2 a summary of your qualifications.
3 a summary of your experience in the construction industry.

Use the following phrases to help you:

I am writing in reply to your advertisement in [name of newspaper/website] for [job title].
I am currently working on …
My main qualifications are …
I started working in the construction industry in …
I believe I have the right experience and qualifications for this job, specifically my …
I look forward to hearing from you in the near future.

2

Design

- describe technical drawings
- estimate
- discuss ideas and improvements
- discuss light tube technology

Technical drawing

Reading **1** Look at three representations of a house. Name the types of drawing. Then read the text and check your answers.

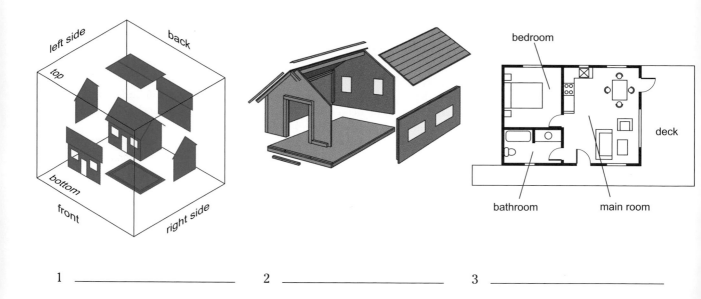

1 _____   2 _____   3 _____

There are many ways of putting a 3D object into 2D. Orthographic projections can be found on all construction projects. These drawings show different views of the object, and can include elevations (a view from one side) and cross-sections (the view when you cut through an object). Another type of drawing shows exploded views, which are very useful for understanding the assembly of an object, in other words how it all fits together. A third type of drawing is the plan view, which allows us to see an object from above. A typical example of this is a floor plan. These are very useful when we want to look at the fittings in detail, in other words where objects like cookers and baths go.

Speaking **2** Work in small groups. Discuss what other types of drawing are used in the construction industry.

Vocabulary **3** Identify these 2D shapes in the drawings in 1. Write the names of the shapes on the drawings.

circle   I-shape   oval   rectangle   square   triangle

4 Work in pairs. Brainstorm objects and equipment on a construction site which are these 3D shapes.

| cone cube cylinder rectangular prism sphere |

5 ▶ ⓪ **05** Listen to an architect describing the house in 1. Write the dimensions you hear.

house – *28 foot long (± 1"), 20 foot wide (± 1")*

1 total area – _____
2 main room, with the kitchen – _____
3 bedroom – _____
4 bathroom – _____
5 height of rooms – _____
6 doors, not including frames – _____

Language

Talking about dimensions

We write:	We say:
Imperial	
12' x 16'	twelve foot (or feet) by sixteen foot (or feet)
560 sq ft (or sq ft)	five hundred and sixty square foot (or feet)
2'8"	two foot (or feet) eight inches
sq yd (or sq yd)	square yard (one square yard = three feet by three feet)
Metric	
1.34 mm	one point three four millimetres
0.03 cm	zero (or nought) point oh three centimetres
25 m²	twenty-five square metres
2,000 m	two thousand metres
We use **plus or minus** to talk about **tolerances:**	
28' ± 1"	twenty-eight foot (or feet) plus or minus one inch
We use **to** to talk about **scales:**	
15:1	fifteen to one

6 Say these dimensions aloud.

1 3.065 mm
2 3'4"
3 34 m x 28 m
4 26' ± ½ "

5 2,500 sq ft
6 4,632 m²
7 0.045 cm

Vocabulary **7** Match 1–5 with their meanings a–e.

1 section
2 elevation
3 scale
4 orthographic projection
5 plan view

a) the view of a building seen from one side
b) the view when you cut through the building
c) the view from above
d) the size of a drawing compared to the original
e) a 2D representation of a 3D object

Speaking **8** Draw the front and side elevations and a plan view of a typical house in your country. Include the dimensions. Describe your drawing to a partner.

9 Draw a floor plan. Include details such as important fittings. Explain your drawing to a partner.

Estimates

Reading **1** What is the surface area of this book? Estimate it and then measure to check. How much does it weigh?

2 Read the text about estimating. Do you agree with it?

> Estimating is at the heart of the construction industry. Estimating is about calculating time, materials, equipment costs and so on. If we overestimate, someone else gets the job. If we underestimate, we lose money. So it's very important that we get it right.

Listening **3** ▶ 🔊 06 Listen to a contractor talking about estimating. Who is he speaking to?

4 Listen again. Complete the contractor's summary of the estimating process.

look at various documents
1 _____ our initial estimate
2 _____ more accurate
3 _____ the profit
4 _____ an estimate

Vocabulary **5** Here are some of the collocations from the listening. Match them and then underline them in audio script 6 on page 71.

1 utility   a) fees
2 relevant   b) estimate
3 initial   c) information
4 subcontractor   d) quotes
5 legal   e) requirements
6 building   f) construction
7 temporary   g) permits

6 Find words in audio script 6 that are similar in meaning to:

1 equipment   _____
2 initial   _____
3 precise   _____
4 indirect costs   _____
5 papers   _____
6 customer   _____
7 offer   _____

Language

Zero conditional	
We use the zero conditional (*if* + present tense + present tense) to say what we think is certain to happen. We think it is a fact.	If we **underestimate**, we **lose** money. (or We **lose** money if we **underestimate**.) If it **snows**, we **can't** work. (or We **can't** work if it **snows**.)

7 Match 1–5 to a–e to make sentences.

1 If the materials are late, we can't	a) need more bricks.
2 If we expect bad weather, we allow	b) of business.
3 If we want a ten-foot wall, we	c) start work.
4 If we don't make a profit, we are out	d) for stoppages.
5 If you have a large project, estimating	e) becomes quite complex.

8 Complete these sentences using your own ideas.

1 If you want to prevent accidents, …
2 If iron gets wet, …
3 If I have a problem, …

Reading **9** Read the email and answer these questions.

1 Who is the email from?
2 Who is the email to?
3 What is the enquiry about?

To: info@martinipools.org
From: f.ali@pjk.com

Dear Mr Martini,

I would like to build a swimming pool in my garden. Please can you contact me to discuss how much it will cost? My telephone number is below.

Many thanks and best regards,

Fareed Ali

10 List the things the contractor needs to find out before producing an estimate.

Listening **11** 🔊 **07** Listen to the conversation about building the swimming pool. Add to your list in 10.

12 Listen again. Answer these questions.

1 How long will the pool be?
2 How deep will it be at the deepest end?
3 Will the pool have steps?
4 What type of ground is on the site?
5 How long will the project take?

Speaking **13** Imagine a friend asks you to help him estimate the costs for building a garage on the side of his house. List the things he needs to consider in his estimate. Then compare ideas with a partner.

dimensions – First of all, we need to know the exact dimensions of the garage.
utilities – We need to check electrical requirements.

Ideas and improvements

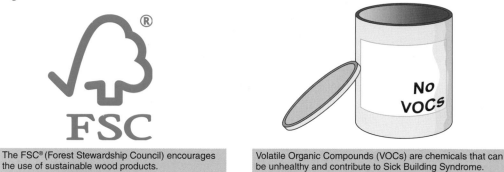

The FSC® (Forest Stewardship Council) encourages the use of sustainable wood products.

Volatile Organic Compounds (VOCs) are chemicals that can be unhealthy and contribute to Sick Building Syndrome.

1 ▶ 🔊 08 Listen to two site managers, Magda and Habib, talking about plans for a new office block. What is the discussion about?

2 Complete the first column in the table. Then tick who is doing each task. Listen again and check your answers.

	Magda	Habib
1 calculations to strengthen the _____		
2 speak to client about _____ the floor		
3 speak to Ahmed about _____		
4 speak to joiners about FSC _____		
5 organise natural _____		
6 speak to HVAC people about _____		

Language **3** Here are some ways Magda and Habib introduce and respond to ideas. Underline them in audio script 8 on page 72. Identify which phrases introduce ideas (I) and which phrases respond (R) to them.

How about if I …?
I know. Why don't we …?
Yes, good idea.
We'll need to …
Maybe we need to …
Yes, that's a good point.
Sure.
Yes, that makes sense. But isn't …?
He's OK with that.
There's no need (to …)

Speaking **4** Work in pairs. Find words in audio script 8 that collocate with these words.
1 natural
2 dividing
3 workstation
4 environmentally
5 energy

5 Use some of the collocations in 4 to discuss improvements to the room you are in. Take turns to introduce an idea and respond to it.

A: Why don't we make the windows bigger to increase the natural lighting?
B: Yes, good idea. But isn't that expensive?

6 Look at this plan of a construction site and read the list of problems with it. Discuss improvements with a partner, then tell the class your ideas.

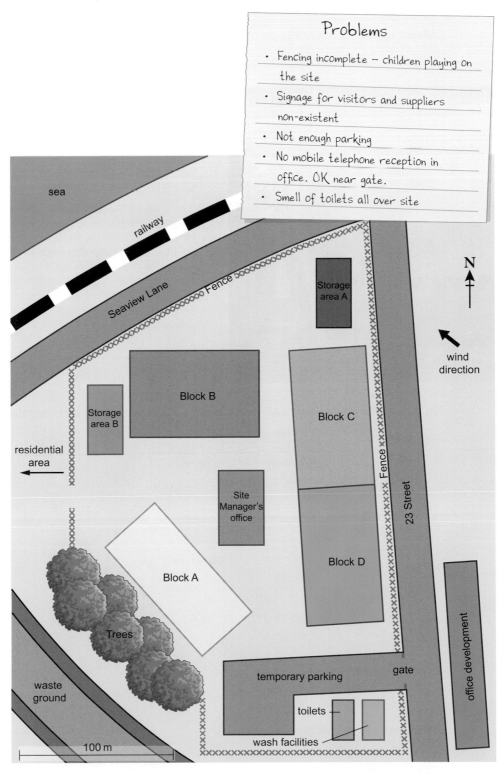

Problems

- Fencing incomplete – children playing on the site
- Signage for visitors and suppliers non-existent
- Not enough parking
- No mobile telephone reception in office. OK near gate.
- Smell of toilets all over site

7 Many construction sites have similar problems due to lack of space and compromises are made. Think of examples from construction sites you know. Work in small groups and tell your group about them.

Focus on a project: Light tubes in Potsdamer Platz, Berlin

Reading **1** Look at the photo. What are the tubes? What do they do?

2 Read the text about the light tubes in Potsdamer Platz. What is a heliostat?

Visitors to Potsdamer Platz in Berlin are often interested to see three glass tubes, up to ten metres high, near the entrance to the underground railway station. The tubes, made of glass and steel, transfer sunlight down into the station.

There are three light tubes, 14 metres, 17 metres and 21 metres in length in total, each with an external diameter of 1 metre. At the top is a heliostat which follows the sun and uses mirrors to reflect the sun's light into the tube, which is lined with a highly reflective material. Inside each tube is a steel pipe, also covered with a reflective material. The light travels down the tube until it reaches a glass cover which allows the light to spread into the station. At night artificial light travels up the tubes and helps to light up Potsdamer Platz.

3 Are these statements true (T) or false (F)? Correct the false statements.

1 Each tube is over ten metres above ground. (T / F)
2 The tubes are made of glass and steel. (T / F)
3 A heliostat contains mirrors. (T / F)
4 Each light tube contains a plastic pipe. (T / F)
5 Light can only travel down the tubes. (T / F)

4 Look at this sketch of a light tube. What do the letters stand for?

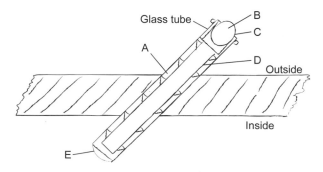

Speaking **5** Work in small groups. Do you think light tubes will be common in the future? Why (not)?

Review

Language **1** Write these dimensions in words.

    1 45.805 cm   5 15' ± ¾"

    2 27' 3"   6 0.045 cm

    3 7,643 sq yd   7 1,267 m^2

    4 17 cm x 13 cm

2 Put these words in the correct order to make zero conditional sentences.

    1 If / need, / you / tell / help / me

    2 If / it / wet / site, / things / on / rains / get

    3 If / visits / the / client / let / know / me

    4 If / is / you / a / cube / cut, / the / a / cross-section / square

    5 If / strike / there / is / a, / stops / work

3 Complete this conversation between two builders. Use one word in each space.

    A: The client thinks that the room is too dark.

    B: No (1) _____ . (2) _____ don't we install more lights?

    A: Well, he wants natural lighting.

    B: I see. How (3) _____ if I make the windows bigger?

    A: But the walls aren't strong enough …

    B: That's a good (4) _____ . I know … why (5) _____ we use light tubes?

    A: Light tubes?

    B: Yes. They come in kits. We'll (6) _____ to cut a hole in the roof first. I think the diameter is about 40 cm. The tube goes from the roof, through the attic and comes out in the ceiling. At the top there's a semi-spherical glass dome which collects the sunlight. This light is reflected down the tube. And at the bottom there's a ceiling-mounted unit which transfers the sunlight into the room.

    A: That makes (7) _____ . But aren't they expensive?

    B: Not really. Around $300, I (8) _____ . They should take around half a day to install.

    A: I'm sure he'll be OK with (9) _____ .

    B: OK. I'll call the office and ask them to produce a proper (10) _____ .

Vocabulary **4** Name the shapes that are 90-degree cross-sections of:

    a cylinder   *a circle; a rectangle*

    1 a cube   _____

    2 a rectangular prism   _____

    3 a sphere   _____

    4 a cone   _____ _____

5 Write the opposites.

    simple   *complex*

    1 permanent   _____

    2 final   _____

    3 subtract   _____

    4 different   _____

    5 hardware   _____

    6 loss   _____

6 Do the following, then compare with your classmates.

    1 Draw a floor plan of your classroom and label the fittings.

    2 Draw the front and side elevations of an object in the room and include dimensions.

3 Equipment • talk about equipment
• explain faults
• deal with repairs
• discuss equipment for a skyscraper project

Talking about equipment

Vocabulary **1** Look at this construction site equipment. Which equipment can you identify?

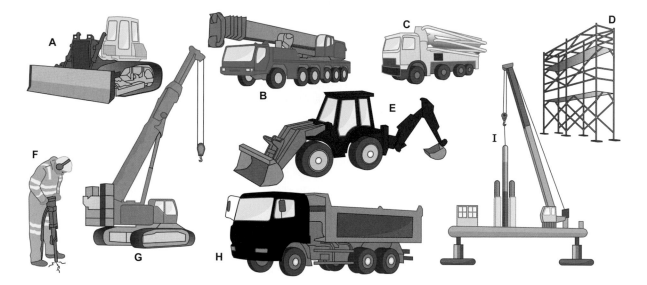

2 Look at the illustration again. Name equipment that:

1 uses hydraulics.   _____
2 has tracks.   _____
3 uses stabilisers.   _____
4 lifts loads.   _____
5 digs trenches.   _____
6 drives piles into the ground. _____
7 breaks things.   _____

Language

Asking and answering questions about equipment

What **does** *a bulldozer* **do**? *What* **do** *bulldozers* **do**?	*It* **moves** *earth.* *They* **move** *earth.*
What **is** *a jackhammer* **for**? *What* **are** *jackhammers* **for**?	*It's* **for** *break**ing** up concrete, rocks, etc.* *They're* **for** *break**ing** up concrete, rocks, etc.*
What **can** *an HP231* **do**? *What* **can** *HP231s* **do**?	*It* **can pump** *30 litres per minute.* *They* **can pump** *30 litres per minute.*
What's it **used for**? *What's it* **used to do**?	*It's* **used for** *moving earth.* *It's* **used to lift** *heavy loads.*
What **do** *you* **use** *this* **for**? *What* **do** *you* **use** *this* **to do**?	*You* **use** *it* **for** *moving earth.* *You* **use** *this* **to move** *earth.*

Listening **3** **🌀 09** Complete the descriptions of construction site equipment. Put one word in each gap. Then listen and check your answers.

1   This machine is _____ driving piles into the soil.
2   This machine has a bucket which is used _____ scoop soil out of the ground.
3   This machine _____ lift heavy loads high in the air.
4   You _____ this machine to move large amounts of earth.
5   This machine _____ electricity from petrol.
6   This machine _____ used for transporting concrete to high parts of a construction site.
7   This machine is _____ to transport people to high parts of a construction site.

4 Match these types of equipment to their descriptions in 3.

a) a crane
b) a lift/an elevator
c) a pile driver
d) a generator
e) a concrete pump/a cement pump
f) a backhoe
g) a bulldozer

Speaking **5** Work in small groups. Brainstorm different ways to use these items.

Reading **6** Read these extracts from manufacturers' sales brochures. Name the types of equipment they describe.

1   We manufacture a complete range of units, including truck and trailer mounted. Great reliability and superb performance. Our largest units can pump up to 160 cubic metres per hour.

2
• Range of up to 25 m
• Rechargeable battery
• State of the art joysticks give precise handling
• Our products are used to control lifting equipment all over the world.

3   Our units come in a variety of sizes and are fully equipped and ready to use. Standard features include steps, office furniture, heating/air conditioning, and interior and exterior lighting.

4   *Made of high quality steel, they are used to transport heavy construction waste, including rubble and other debris. All models have large lifting eyes and a sloped end to make load discharge easy.*

Speaking **7** Work in pairs. Discuss equipment you are familiar with or are training to use.

A: *I use a jackhammer in my job.*
B: *What do you use it for?*
A: *You use it for breaking up concrete.*

Faults

1 Read the maintenance checklist. Identify the piece of equipment it refers to.

Daily inspection checklist

Inspector: _____ Date: _____ Time: _____

Vehicle/Plant identification number: _____

✓ = OK   O = *keep under observation*   R = *replace/repair*   N/A = *not applicable*

	ITEM	CHECK FOR	COMMENTS
Safety	fire extinguisher	damage	
	first aid kit	contents	
	triangle	damage	
	ROPS*	damage	
Cab	glass/mirrors	damage, cleanliness	
	horn/lights	function	
	wipers	wear, function	
	seat/seat belt	damage, function	
	heater	function	
Engine	engine oil	level, leaks	
	hoses	damage, leaks	
	belts	wear, looseness	
	battery	damage, cleanliness	
Other	general	loose/missing bolts or fixtures, damage, cleanliness	
	fluid reservoirs	levels, leaks	
	hydraulics	wear, damage, leaks	
	bucket	wear, edge, cleanliness	

* Roll Over Protection System

Listening **2** ▶ 10 Listen to two engineers going through the checklist in 1. Make notes and then complete the *Comments* column. Use O or R from the key as necessary.

3 Listen again. Write simple sentences to explain the meaning of these sentences and phrases.

1 A couple of things.   _____
2 I tightened it.   _____
3 Anything else?   _____
4 I'll speak to the security people.   _____
5 Got a torch handy?   _____
6 Mohammed's off sick.   _____
7 Tell Farid it's urgent.   _____

Language

The passive with *be* and *get*	
We often use the **be** passive (**be** + past participle) to show the state of something.	The mirror **is cracked**. The hose **is damaged**.
We often use the **get** passive (**get** + past participle) to explain how things happened.	It **got fixed** yesterday. They **got broken** when we moved the box.
get + adjective Note that we also use **get** followed by an adjective to talk about how things happened.	It **got loose**. How did it **get wet**?

4 Complete the sentences with the correct form of the verb in brackets.

1 The wiper got _____ (break).
2 The hoses are _____ (wear).
3 The horn is _____ (fix).
4 The reservoir got _____ (damage).
5 The rear brake light is _____ (crack).

5 Are these statements true (T) or false (F)? Correct the false statements.

1 A mirror can get broken. (T / F)
2 A manual can get wet. (T / F)
3 A hose can get updated. (T / F)
4 A backhoe can't get painted. (T / F)
5 A trench can't get built. (T / F)

6 Match 1–5 to a–e to make sentences.

1 The cup? It got broken
2 The manual? It got updated
3 The new total station? It got damaged
4 The tank? It got filled up at
5 The hydraulic fluid? It got checked

a) yesterday. Sam said he put in half a litre.
b) in transit. There was too much vibration.
c) when I was making tea. I dropped it.
d) last year. That's an old version.
e) the petrol station before we left.

7 Complete these conversations using *get*, *gets* or *got*.

1 How did the windscreen _____ cracked?   By some stones.
  He was driving too fast.
2 Where's my sandwich?   It _____ eaten.
3 Why didn't you phone?   My phone _____ wet.
  I dropped it in a puddle.
4 Why was John late?   He _____ lost.
5 Why are you packing up?   It _____ dark at five.
6 How did it _____ damaged?   I'm not sure, probably in transit.

Speaking **8** Work in pairs to talk about a damaged piece of equipment. Student A: Use the information below. Student B: Turn to page 68.

Student A: Use all the words in the box. Decide what happened to the wheelbarrow.

| bent | broken | bumper | dent | hit | truck | wheel | wheelbarrow |

Repairs

Speaking **1** What's the difference between *maintain* and *repair*? Give examples.

Listening **2** 🔘 **11** Listen to a supervisor giving instructions about some repairs to an office trailer. Make notes about the repairs that need doing.

3 Listen again. Who is doing each task? Complete the table.

NAME	TASK
John	(1) _____
	(2) _____
	(3) _____
(4) _____	(5) _____
	grease the jack
Supervisor	(6) _____

Vocabulary **4** Write the phrase:

1 the supervisor uses to explain that he is giving instructions.
2 the supervisor uses to describe a quick task.
3 the supervisor uses to say that he will do the work.
4 Sandra uses to explain that the welding will take no more than sixty minutes.

5 Use the phrases in 4 to complete this conversation.

José:	Excuse me, are you the supervisor?
Supervisor:	Yes, that's right.
José:	I'm José, the carpenter's apprentice. Mr Rodrigo said you had a job for me. He said (1) _____ .
Supervisor:	Ah, yes, but not an hour. (2) _____ .
José:	OK, good.
Supervisor:	You see the electricians over there? Well, they've just installed a new system. They want to test it. (3) _____ : I need you to stand on the other side of the building. You'll see a grey box on the wall. When you're in position, I'll raise my hand. They'll switch everything on and you check that the green lights come on, OK?
José:	Yes, OK. And what about this documentation for the electricians?
Supervisor:	(4) _____ . Just get in position now.
José:	OK.

6 Read the operating instructions for a piece of equipment. Is it a) a portable generator, b) a pile driver or c) a bulldozer?

1	Make sure the unit is on level ground.
2	Open the fuel cock.
3	Open the choke to FULL.
4	Pull the starting rope slowly until you feel resistance.
5	Pull the starting rope hard and fast.
6	When the unit is running, move choke lever to RUN.

7 Read the troubleshooting (fault finding) guide for the equipment in 6. Match the problem to a possible cause and to the corrective action.

PROBLEM	POSSIBLE CAUSE	CORRECTIVE ACTION
1 engine turns, but fails to start	no coolant	clean fuel lines
2 engine does not turn	no fuel	replace pressure gauge
3 low oil pressure	flat battery	check for leaks
4 engine misfires	blocked fuel lines	fill up fuel tank
5 engine overheats	faulty pressure gauge	charge or replace battery

8 🔊 12 Complete these sentences with the words in the box. Then listen and check your answers.

> gauge lights misfiring reservoir start turning

1 I can't get the genny to _____ . The engine is _____ over, so the battery must be all right.
2 There's a problem with the JCB. The temperature _____ is showing red.
3 Listen to the bulldozer. The engine is _____ . Any ideas what it could be?
4 Have you seen the mechanic? The gauge is showing low pressure, but the oil _____ is full.
5 Can you look at the crane, please? It's completely dead. There are no _____ , nothing.

Need to/need + -ing

We use *need* in different ways, depending on where we want to put the emphasis.	We **need to** sort out the trailer. The trailer **needs** sorting out.

9 Read audio script 11 on page 73. Underline the phrases with *need*. Notice how the word is used.

10 Use the troubleshooting guide in 7 to give solutions to the problems in 8.

1 The fuel tank is empty. We need to fill it up./ The tank needs filling up.

11 Choose one of the repairs that need doing to the office trailer on page 24 and explain to a partner how to do it.

The broken hinge needs replacing, so first you need to …

12 Read audio script 11 on page 73 between the supervisor and his team. Roleplay a similar situation with your classmates.

Focus on a project: The Shard, London

Reading

The Shard is a skyscraper in the centre of London, just near the famous Tower Bridge. It is one of the tallest buildings in Europe. Designed by Renzo Piano, the tower has 88 levels and is clad entirely in glass. It contains offices, restaurants, bars, cafés, viewing galleries, a hotel and residential apartments. One of the biggest challenges the developers had to deal with was to minimise disruption in the local area: The Shard is located next to London Bridge station, one of the busiest transport hubs in London, and Guy's Hospital, a large teaching hospital. Noise and dust had to be kept to a minimum. On this page you will look at some of the equipment that was used in the construction of The Shard.

1   These cantilever loading platforms are easy to install and move. Cranes lift the platforms into position. They are flush with the floor allowing the movement of large objects in and out of the structure.

2   High-rise buildings like the Shard need a lot of concrete. This project used a powerful, high-performance pump which can pump more than 90m³ of concrete per hour.

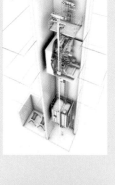

3   Normally a lift shaft has to be complete before a lift can be installed. With jump lift technology this is not necessary. As the building rises, the jump lift, which contains its own machine room, rises with it.

4   The Shard construction site used a number of cranes. The lead crane in the centre occupied the highest spot. This crane was mounted inside the core. As the building rose the crane was jacked up.

Vocabulary   **1**   Read the text and look at the photos. Find words which are close in meaning to these words.

1   simple   5   tall
2   on the same level as   6   middle
3   elevator   7   uppermost
4   finished

Speaking   **2**   Think about the four pieces of equipment mentioned in the texts. What are they for? Make notes and discuss your ideas with a partner.

3   How do you think the top crane was removed at the end of the construction phase?

4   Find photos of The Shard construction site on the internet. Can you identify any other pieces of equipment? Report back to the class. Explain what the equipment is for.

Review

1 Read these two conversations about maintenance. Complete them with the words in the box.

| battery | damaged | dirt | grease | hose | tank |

Conversation 1
A: What are we going to do about the leak?
B: Do you mean the leak in the (1) _____ ?
A: Yes.
B: Well, it's just a small leak. I think we can top up the (2) _____ with hydraulic oil, and keep an eye on it.
A: OK. And the cracked (3) _____ ?
B: Let's try glue.
A: Glue?
B: Yes, it's only the casing. It should be OK.
A: Fine, but it could be (4) _____ inside.
B: That's true. Let's replace it then.

Conversation 2
A: I greased all the Zerk fittings on the backhoe. They needed it. There was lots of (1) _____.
B: Thanks. I normally do them every morning, but I was too busy this morning.
A: Any idea why they're called Zerk fittings?
B: A guy called Zerk invented them, I think. You can also call them (2) _____ fittings. It makes more sense.
A: Yes.

Language **2** Answer these questions.

1 What is hydraulic oil used for?
2 What do batteries do?
3 What are Zerk fittings for?

3 Write these sentences in another way so that the emphasis changes.

We need to sort out the delivery.   *The delivery needs sorting out.*
1 We need to improve the quality of the concrete.
2 We need to revise the schedule.
3 We need to cover the sand before it starts to rain.
4 We need to inspect the wiring.
5 We need to go through the contract.
6 We need to fill in the trench by 5 p.m.

4 Correct the errors with *get* in these sentences.

Let's pack up. It get dark at around six.   *Let's pack up. It **gets** dark at around six.*
1 The paperwork gets all wet when it rained.
2 The pipe gets fixed yesterday.
3 The oil tank get damaged in the accident.
4 An extinguisher get stolen every week.
5 How did it got cracked?
6 Where were you when he get fired?

Writing **5** Choose one of these pieces of equipment. Write down five things you should check regularly as part of a maintenance programme.

| backhoe | bulldozer | cement pump | crane | fork lift truck | generator |

4 Materials

- order materials
- describe properties of materials
- explain delivery problems
- discuss problems and solutions involving materials

Ordering materials

Reading **1** Read the four texts. Decide the order they were written in.

Torano Ltd
Plumbing Supplies

DELIVERY NOTE	CONSIGNOR'S COPY
Supplier: *Torano Ltd, Plumbing Supplies, Ras Al Khor Industrial Area*	Date: *17 May* Reference: *HU 23/67*
Customer address: *Al Jadaf Avenue 456*	Customer Identification Number: *2675L*
Delivery address: *Jumeirah Street 23A*	
Transport: *Truck* Shipping Agent: *Shonker*	
Order number: *3728*	Total weight: *34 kg*
Description: *Pipes HT-670*	Value: *289.07 AED*
Delivered by:	Quantity: *4 m*
Name (BLOCK CAPS): *ALI HAMAD*	
Received:	
I certify the above items were received in good order and condition.	Date: *17/5* Time: *12:25*
Name (BLOCK CAPS): *GHAD*	Signature: *Ghad*

Pls ask Torano 2
send quote
for 4 m pipe
HT-675. Delivery
Jumeirah Str site
17 May.
thx.

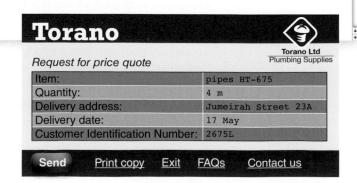

Dear Ms Sarkis,

Thank you for your request for a price quote. Unfortunately the pipes you requested are not in stock at the moment. However we can offer you other similar pipes for the same price. A copy of the specifications is attached. Please let us know your decision.

Alfredo Torano

Manager

Torano

Torano Ltd
Plumbing Supplies

Request for price quote

Item:	pipes HT-675
Quantity:	4 m
Delivery address:	Jumeirah Street 23A
Delivery date:	17 May
Customer Identification Number:	2675L

Send   Print copy   Exit   FAQs   Contact us

Vocabulary **2** Match the terms in 1–7 with their meanings a–g. Use the texts in 1 to help you.

1 BLOCK CAPS
2 price quote
3 in stock
4 FAQs
5 signature
6 delivery note
7 request

a) a document from the seller to the buyer, giving details of a delivery
b) ask for
c) information about how much the goods cost
d) a person's name, written in his/her own handwriting
e) CAPITAL LETTERS
f) Frequently Asked Questions
g) The seller has the items in his store.

3 Find words in the texts in 1 that are similar in meaning to thcsc words.

1 goods   _____
2 number   _____
3 value   _____
4 seller   _____
5 lorry   _____
6 client   _____
7 details _____

Language

The passive	
In an active sentence, the subject is the 'doer' who performs the action of the verb. In a **passive** sentence, the object of the active verb becomes the subject.	*Ms Sarkis **ordered** the goods.* (active) *The goods **were ordered** by Ms Sarkis.* (passive)
We use the **passive** when the 'doer' is unknown or unimportant, or when the 'doer' is obvious. We form the passive with an appropriate form of *be* + past participle.	*This equipment **is made** in Germany.* *The packages **were sent** last week.*

4 Complete these sentences with information from the texts in 1.

1 The name of the seller is _____ .
2 The goods were ordered by _____ .
3 The goods cost _____ .
4 The goods were delivered to _____ (address).
5 The goods were delivered by _____ (name).
6 The goods were signed for by _____ .
7 The goods were delivered at _____ (time).

5 Read this text about one of the greatest construction projects in history. Complete it with the correct passive form of the verbs in brackets.

The Great Pyramid of Giza (1) _____ (*design*) as a tomb for an Egyptian Pharaoh. Many people think it (2) _____ (*construct*) using slave labour, but we have no real evidence of this. The pyramid has changed over the years. For example, it (3) _____ originally _____ (*cover*) in casing stones, but these (4) _____ (*remove*) by later generations. The pyramid contains at least three chambers. The lowest is under the pyramid and (5) _____ (*cut*) into the rock. It (6) _____ never _____ (*finish*). The other chambers (7) _____ (*build*) into the pyramid itself.

Speaking **6** Work in pairs. Think of a construction site you know. How are building materials ordered? What paperwork is required? Give examples.

Properties of materials

Speaking **1** Work in pairs. Imagine you are going to build a driveway to a house. Think about the materials and the different layers you will need. Give reasons for your choices. Use these sketches to help you.

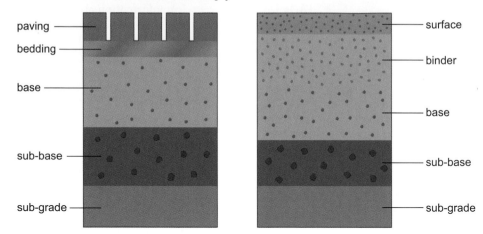

Listening **2** 🔊 **13** Listen to a contractor describing two types of driveway construction. List the materials you hear.

stones, …

3 Here are some adjectives (in italics) that the contractor uses to describe the materials. Write the opposite of the adjectives. Then listen again and check your answers.

1 a *firm* surface ＿＿＿＿＿＿＿
2 *coarse* sand or grit ＿＿＿＿＿＿＿
3 a *strong* sub-base ＿＿＿＿＿＿＿
4 *tough* edging ＿＿＿＿＿＿＿
5 an *attractive* appearance ＿＿＿＿＿＿＿
6 a *rough* texture ＿＿＿＿＿＿＿

4 🔊 **14** Listen to a contractor talking about the key properties of asphalt. Make notes on what he says about the following.

penetration value – *tells you how hard or soft the asphalt is; depends on the climate*
1 cutback
2 porosity
3 noise reduction
4 reflection

5 Match these words to the key properties in 4. Listen again and check your answers.

| cure | glare | hard | sound | water |

Speaking **6** Work in pairs. Discuss why the properties in 4 are important in building roads.
Penetration values tell us how hard or soft the asphalt is. I think harder asphalt lasts longer, but in hot climates hard asphalt cracks.

7 Match the nouns 1–6 with the correct adjectives a–f.

1 strength   a) elastic
2 toughness   b) strong
3 hardness   c) brittle
4 elasticity   d) porous
5 brittleness   e) hard
6 porosity   f) tough

8 Complete these sentences by choosing the correct words in *italics*.

1 Asphalt is used in road construction because it is *strength / strong*.
2 *Hardness / Hard* asphalt is often very *brittleness / brittle*.
3 *Porosity / Porous* asphalt improves safety by removing water from the surface of the road.
4 *Toughness / Tough* is a measure of the energy you need to break something.
5 It is important that roads have enough *elasticity / elastic* to return to their original shape after loading.

Language

Comparatives	
We use **adjectives** to describe nouns.	*a **loose**/**firm** surface* *an **original** shape* *a **strong** material*
We make **comparisons** by changing the adjective.	Short adjectives: *hard – **harder**, strong – **stronger*** Adjectives ending in -y: *heavy – **heavier**, easy – **easier*** Long adjectives: *brittle – **more**/**less brittle**, porous – **more**/**less porous***

9 Complete these sentences with materials of your choice.

1 A rubber band is more elastic than _____ .
2 A ceramic tile is more brittle than _____ .
3 A piece of steel is harder than _____ .
4 Soil is more porous than _____ .
5 A slab of concrete is stronger than _____ .
6 A piece of Kevlar® is tougher than _____ .

10 What building material(s) can be used to complete all of the sentences in 9?

Speaking 11 Scaffolding can be constructed using different materials, such as metal pipes or bamboo. With a partner, list the properties of these two materials and discuss the advantages and disadvantages of each.

Delivery problems

Speaking **1** Look at these illustrations. Discuss what the problem is in each.

Listening **2** 🔊 **15** Listen to three conversations about delivery problems. Identify the problem in each.

Conversation 1 _____

Conversation 2 _____

Conversation 3 _____

3 Read the information from Conversation 1. Listen again and correct the four mistakes.

Caller:	Abdulla	Goods arrived:	9:00
Company:	Kawasoki Construction	Goods signed for by:	Malik Zahid
Order number:	G2356-J	Delivery address:	12 Bridge Road
Goods dispatched	10:05		

4 Imagine you are the caller in Conversation 2. Listen again and complete the sentences to summarise the problem.

1 I'm calling about …
2 You sent the wrong …
3 We ordered …
4 You sent …

5 Listen again to Conversation 3. Where is the truck? Choose the correct sketch.

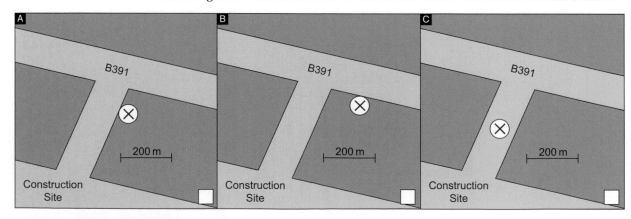

Language **6** Complete these questions from audio script 15 on page 74.

1 _____ I just confirm your company name, please?
2 _____ it the wrong sand?
3 What _____ you mean?
4 So _____ you saying that we sent you three truckloads?
5 _____ is the sand now?
6 _____ you say unloaded?
7 _____ you repeat that, please?

7 Match the problems 1–7 with the responses a–g.

1 The rebar we ordered hasn't arrived. The order number is 235688.
2 You sent us a bill for $3,000. It should be $300.
3 You sent us a bill for $3,000. We paid it last week.
4 We need another bag of cement. Do you have any in stock?
5 We ordered 14 XAFs. You only sent us 12.
6 The catalogue number on the package is different to the one on the delivery note.
7 The catalogue number on the package is different to the one on the item.

a) It sounds like we put the wrong items in the box.
b) Just ignore it. Sorry about that.
c) I'll sort it out now and send you a new bill today.
d) I think so, yes. Let me check and I'll get back to you. What's your number?
e) Did you say rebar? Just one moment, please. I'll put you through to the right department.
f) It sounds like the driver gave you the wrong package … or the wrong paperwork.
g) We'll send you two more this afternoon.

Asking for clarification	
Ask the other person to repeat.	*Could you repeat that, please?* *Could you say that again?* *Pardon?*
Say it again in your own words.	*Just to clarify, …* *Do you mean that …?* *So are you saying that …?* *Did you say …?*
Ask for more details.	*What do you mean?* *Could you clarify that?*

Speaking **8** Work in pairs. Roleplay the situations in audio script 15 on page 74.

1 Student A: You are Abdulla. Phone Malik Zahid and tell him what happened. Solve the problem.
Student B: You are Malik Zahid. Take the call.
2 Student A: You are Christina Dudek. Phone a colleague and ask for suggestions about how to solve the sand delivery problem.
Student B: You are Christina Dudek's colleague. Help her solve her problem.
3 Student A: You are Alano Baldamero. Call one of your supervisors and ask him to send a crew to pull out the truck that's stuck.
Student B: You are a supervisor working for Alano Baldamero. Take the call. Make sure you have all the details you need.

9 Do you know any stories about wrong deliveries? What happened? Share them with the class.

Focus on a project: Bahrain International Circuit Formula 1 (BIC)

Reading Bahrain International Circuit (BIC) was completed in 2004 and is now used as a venue for different racing events, including Formula 1. It cost approximately US$150 million to build. One of the most interesting features of the track is its desert location, which created interesting challenges for the designers.

1 Read the text about the quantities of materials used in the construction of Bahrain International Circuit. Complete it with the figures in the box.

40,509 m²	400,000 litres	600	70,000 m³	8,500 tonnes

The construction of the circuit was carried out in record time for such a huge project. It was completed in just 485 days – from concept to race. It required 8,265,000 man hours, 2,084 workers, (1) _____ of sweet water, 300,000 hollow blocks, 190,810 m³ paving bricks, 820,000 m³ rock removing, 300,000 m³ asphalt, (2) _____ concrete, 1,000 tonnes aluminium, (3) _____ steel, 7,750 m² glass, 30,000 m electric wiring, 70,000 timing circuitry, 78,919 m² paint, (4) _____ plaster, 10,800 m² roofing membrane and finally (5) _____ palm trees.

2 Read the text again. Find examples of building materials for these categories: painting and decorating; electrical; landscaping; masonry.

Speaking **3** After completion, the track was surrounded by artificial grass. What problem does that solve? Choose from this list. Which materials in the text solve the other two problems?

1 It speeds up construction time.
2 It stops sand blowing onto the track.
3 It helps to keep the buildings cool inside.

4 Work in pairs. Student A: Turn to page 69.
Student B: Turn to page 68.

Review

Vocabulary **1** Match the materials 1–5 to their properties a–e.

1 rubber
2 sand
3 reinforced concrete
4 ceramic tiles
5 sandpaper

a) rough
b) porous
c) brittle
d) elastic
e) strong

Language **2** Put these sentences into the passive.

1 We ordered the parts.
2 They sent us the wrong items.
3 The supplier gave him the wrong number.
4 A truck delivered the heaviest box.
5 Abdul signed the paperwork.

3 Put these words in the correct order to make questions and sentences about delivery problems.

1 late / Did / say / you / ?
2 please / Could / you / that / repeat / ?
3 you / exactly / mean / do / What / ?
4 Are / deliver / you / that / saying / you / can't / today / ?
5 Who / please / speaking / am / I / to / ?
6 problem / I'm / about / a / calling / delivery
7 problems / call / again / if / I / any / have / I'll

Writing **4** Imagine you have just received spare parts for a generator by motorbike courier. Complete the delivery note.

	DELIVERY NOTE	CONSIGNOR'S COPY
Generator Experts Supplies	Supplier: *Generator Experts* *Block 4* *Halid Road*	Date: Reference: *FDZ*
	Customer Address:	Customer Identification Number: *36728*
	Delivery Address:	
	Order number: *36765*	Total weight: *2 kg*
	Description:	Value: *$234.56*
	Delivered by:	Quantity:
	Name (BLOCK CAPS): *K HANI*	
	Received:	
	I certify the above items were received in good order and condition.	Date: Time:
	Name (BLOCK CAPS):	Signature:

Processes

- sequence events
- plan a process
- explain changes
- discuss emergency housing construction

Setting out

Speaking **1** Work in small groups and answer the questions.

1 What is a straight line? Try to agree on a clear definition.
2 What is the easiest way of setting out a straight line on a construction site?

Listening **2** ▶ 🕑 16 Listen to a surveyor describing the process of setting out a straight line. Mark the following on the illustration.

1 the observer
2 the assistant
3 a ranging pole
4 a plumb line

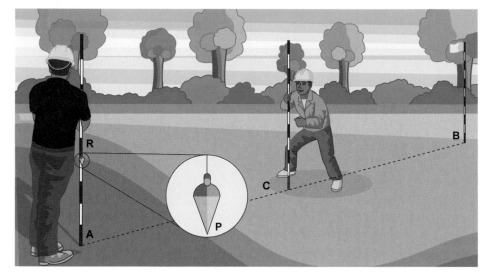

3 Use these prompts to make notes about the process of setting out a straight line. Listen again and check your answers.

1 plans and drawings
2 equipment
3 poles
4 plumb lines
5 assistant
6 pegs

Vocabulary **4** A process is a series of actions that are done in order to achieve a particular result. Explain the difference between *process* and *project*.

5 Match the words in bold in 1–5 with the words or phrases in a–e.

1 This is a **routine** job – we do it every day.
2 What's the **procedure** for setting out?
3 There are three **stages** in the process.
4 The **result** is a straight line.
5 It's important to be **systematic**.

a) outcome
b) steps
c) normal
d) standard way of operating
e) organised

Language

6 Complete this text with the words in the box.

> Finally   First   result   routine   stages   Third

We do this every day: it's (1) _____ . The procedure is simple. There are only seven (2) _____ and the (3) _____ is always the same. (4) _____ , you smile at the guard and say 'Good morning'. Second, the guard smiles back and says 'Good morning'. (5) _____ , the guard asks you for your ID. After showing him your ID, the guard smiles and says 'Thank you'. Then you also smile and say 'Thank you'. (6) _____ , you enter the site.

Speaking   **7** Work in pairs. Take turns to use the flowchart to explain the process of painting a house.

First, you need to clean …

caulk = to fill in the holes to keep water out

scrape = to remove sth from a surface using a sharp object

exposed = not covered, not protected

primer = paint that you put on wood, metal, etc. before the main layer of paint

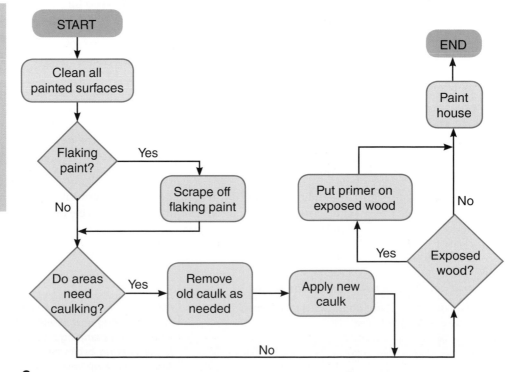

8 Work in pairs to explain other processes you know about. Choose one and draw a flowchart. Then explain the process to another pair.

Recruiting processes

Speaking **1** How do organisations recruit new employees? Give some examples.

Listening **2** ▶ 🔘 **17** Listen to the conversation about recruiting a new structural engineer and answer these questions.

1 Why do Susanne and Peter need a new structural engineer?
2 What is the meeting on Monday about?

3 Put the stages of the recruitment process in the correct order. Listen again and check your answers.

advertise externally	
advertise internally	
carry out interviews	
check CVs	
check references	
identify key skills	*1*
inform applicant	
make decision	
organise induction	
prepare/update job description	
produce shortlist	

Vocabulary **4** Change these verbs to nouns. Then complete the exchanges with the nouns.

advertise   inform   organise   prepare   produce   update

Conversation 1
A: Here are the (1) _____ you asked for.
B: Thank you. I'm sorry it's a bit of a rush. There's never enough time for
(2) _____ .

Conversation 2
A: What can you tell me about the (1) _____ ?
B: Well, they only have one (2) _____ . They make the project management software we use.

Conversation 3
A: We need to put an (1) _____ in the newspaper.
B: No problem. I've already written the new job description, and included all the (2) _____ .

Speaking **5** Explain how the recruitment process is different for hiring unskilled labourers on a short-term, casual or temporary basis. Give examples from your own experience.

Language

Present continuous to talk about the future

We can use the **present continuous** to talk about fixed arrangements in the future.	*I'm seeing* the client tomorrow. *We're meeting* next Monday at three o'clock. When *is* she *planning* to leave? *Is* she *coming back* after she has the baby? *Are* you *working* next week? *I'm not travelling* next month.

6 Match questions 1–5 with the correct responses a–e.

1 What are you doing tomorrow?
2 Aren't you going on leave next week?
3 When are you visiting the site?
4 How are you getting there?
5 Who are you going with?

a) Nobody. I'm going on my own.
b) No, I'm not. Not any more. It was cancelled.
c) I'm going on my motorbike.
d) Later this afternoon.
e) I'm travelling to Cairo. I'm having a meeting with a supplier.

7 Answer these questions so that they are true for you.

1 What time are you going home today?
2 What are you eating this evening?
3 When are you going to bed?

Writing **8** Action an email. Choose either A or B.

A You work for a building contractor. Read and then action the email from your boss.

> As you know, we have recently recruited a new member of staff for the office. Like you, he is a _____ *(write your own job title here)*. Although he is very experienced in the construction industry, he only speaks English. As you are one of the best English speakers in the company, I would like you to look after the induction process, which should take no more than three days. Please draw up a programme showing the key topics you think we should cover and send it to me by the end of the day. Include a list of the people you think he should meet.

B You are a student. Read and then action the email from one of your teachers.

> As you know, we have recently received a new intake of students at _____ *(write the name of your college here)*. One of the new students only speaks English. As you are one of the best English speakers in the college, I would like you to look after him for the first few days. Please draw up an induction programme showing what parts of the college you will show him and send it to me by the end of the day. Include a list of the people you think he should meet and things he should know.

Speaking **9** Work in pairs. Explain the process you followed to get to your present position.

I found out about this course/job from a friend. First, I wrote a letter of application. Then I ...

10 Work in pairs or small groups. Explain one of these processes. Give examples from your own experience.

> applying for a training course   applying for leave
> claiming expenses   getting a part-time job   induction

Purchasing processes

Reading **1** Read this text about purchasing. Then explain in your own words the difference between a purchase order, a delivery note and an invoice.

All contractors have processes which cover the various purchasing needs of a project, for example, for buying materials or renting equipment. Most systems deal with three main types of document:

1 Purchase Order

The PO is a written contract between the buyer and the seller. It provides details about the purchased item and is usually necessary when the amount goes over a pre-arranged level. The contractor sends a copy to the supplier authorising the delivery.

2 Delivery Note

Also known as a packing slip, this document gives details of what was actually delivered.

3 Invoice

Invoices are sent from the seller to the buyer and list the products or services supplied, the amount to be paid and the payment terms. The purchase order number and the delivery note number may also be included on the invoice.

Listening **2** ▶ **18** Listen to a contractor explaining how his company handled invoices in the past. Complete the flowchart.

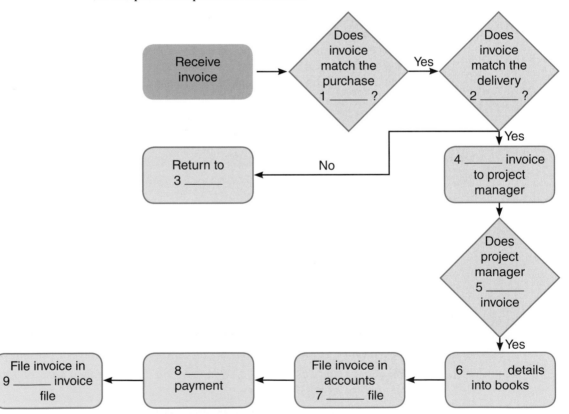

3 Answer these questions. Then listen again and check your answers.

1 Who sent the invoice?
2 Who matched the invoice with the purchase order?
3 Who approved the invoice?
4 Who entered the details of the invoice into the books?
5 Who filed the invoice in the accounts payable file?

4 Match 1–6 with a–f to make collocations.

1	packing	a)	payable
2	delivery	b)	transfer
3	payment	c)	terms
4	purchase	d)	slip
5	accounts	e)	order
6	bank	f)	note

Listening **5** ▶ 🎧 **19** Listen to the contractor explaining how his company handles invoices *now*. Answer these questions.

1 What has changed?
2 What are the advantages?

6 Write the four things the accounts department enter onto the system when they receive an invoice. Then listen again and check your answers.

1 _____
2 _____
3 _____
4 _____

Language

Used to

We use ***used to*** when we want to talk about past routines which are no longer true in the present.	*When I was an apprentice, I **used to** work eight hours a day. Now I work twelve hours.* *We **used to** match each invoice to its purchase order and delivery note by hand. Now the computer does it.*
Negative	*We **didn't use to** wear hard hats on site.* *They **didn't use to** have so many projects overseas.*
Questions	***Did** you **use to** go to work by bus?* *No, I **used to** walk. There were no buses.* *What **did** you **use to** do at lunchtime?* *We **used to** go to the restaurant round the corner.*

7 Underline the examples of *used to* in audio scripts 18 and 19 on page 76.

8 Write three things people in the construction industry *used to do/didn't use to do* before computers.

*They **used to do** all the calculations by hand.*
*They **didn't use to file** documents electronically.*

Speaking **9** Draw a flowchart to show how the company in audio script 19 on page 76 now handles invoices. Then work in pairs and explain the process to your partner. Compare flowcharts.

10 Work in pairs. Explain how things have changed in your workplace or how your lifestyle has changed over the last few years.

People used to use typewriters to write letters. Today we use computers to send emails.
I used to walk to college every day. Now I ride my motorbike.

Focus on a project: Emergency housing

Speaking **1** Work in small groups. Think about some recent, large-scale natural disasters (e.g. earthquakes, floods). Brainstorm factors you think are important in the construction of post-disaster housing.

transportation *of emergency housing to disaster zone*

Reading **2** In two groups, read the articles about emergency housing in China and Japan. Group A: Read Article A. Group B: Read Article B. Then in A/B pairs compare the words in your article that mean:

1 at the same time
2 movable
3 a building used for storage of materials

Article A

Modular construction methods are becoming more and more popular in many parts of the world and are often used in emergency house construction. The prefabrication can be carried out concurrently with the site preparation, allowing significant savings in terms of cost and also of time. The photo shows prefabricated buildings erected to house earthquake victims in Sichuan Province in China in 2008. In such buildings, modules are either delivered almost ready to use or are assembled on site. Larger span structures such as warehouses often make use of steel frameworks. Walls are typically made of expanded polystyrene (EPS) sandwich panels. Another variation is to use mobile homes, which can be transported to different locations and reused as necessary.

Article B

The supply of food and medicine is vital after any natural disaster, but relief organisations also need to simultaneously provide shelter for the survivors. There are many possible solutions, including using shipping containers, tents and plastic sheeting. Often survivors are housed in large buildings such as storehouses or schools and so simple walls are needed to divide up areas into smaller, private spaces. After the 2011 tsunami in Japan, one way Japanese companies solved the problem was to make partitions out of materials such as paper and cardboard. In some cases, whole houses were built out of cardboard. These houses are very portable, cheap and quick to erect, but need to be covered in plastic sheeting if they are to stand up to the weather.

Speaking **3** Work in pairs and discuss these questions. Refer to the article you read in 2.

1 What natural disaster does the article mention?
2 What type of emergency housing does the article describe?
3 What construction materials were used?

4 Imagine a natural disaster in your country. Your company warehouse is full of old shipping containers that victims could use as emergency housing. Many employees have volunteered to help and the company director has agreed to cover costs. Discuss the process you need to follow to get the containers to the disaster area and in use as emergency housing.

Review

Vocabulary **1** Put the activities in a small-scale residential construction project in the correct order. Then write a short text explaining the process.

construction	design	handover	occupancy	site preparation

1 design	→	2	→	3	→	4	→	5

2 Produce a flowchart for modular house construction using the same activities as in 1.

3 Circle the word on the right that is closest in meaning to the word on the left.

1	simultaneous	same / concurrent / equal
2	result	outcome / end / finish
3	preparation	design / planning / process
4	routine	normal / rare / unusual
5	update	inform / instruct / explain
6	mobile	movable / modular / prefabricated
7	warehouse	shelter / container / storehouse

Language **4** Complete this conversation using the present continuous (with future meaning) form of the verbs in brackets.

A: What (1) _____ (you/do) tomorrow? (2) _____ (you/meet) the clients?

B: Yes, that's right. They (3) _____ (arrive) around nine o'clock. I (4) _____ (give) a presentation first and then I (5) _____ (take) them to the site.

A: How (6) _____ (you/get) there? By car?

B: No, there are seven people in the group, so I (7) _____ (use) the minibus.

A: What (8) _____ (you/show) them? The foundations?

B: Yes. And then we (9) _____ (go) over to the storage area to look at the glass panels.

A: Where (10) _____ (you/have) lunch? I might join you.

B: In the restaurant opposite the site – the Italian.

A: What time?

B: One o'clock.

A: Great!

5 Complete this text with the words in the box.

be	give	have	shout	sing	sms	worry

When I was an apprentice, things used to (1) _____ very different. First of all, we didn't use to (2) _____ each other all the time. There weren't any mobile phones in those days. I remember my first site manager – he was a hard man. He used to (3) _____ us dirty jobs if we were late. And he used to (4) _____ at us all the time. We didn't use to (5) _____ so much about health and safety either: no hard hats, no gloves, no reflective vests. We just did the job. But we also used to (6) _____ a lot of fun. I remember we used to (7) _____ while we worked. You never hear that now.

Writing **6** Think of a process at work (or at college) that you are familiar with. Write an email to a new colleague (or to a new student) explaining the key stages.

6 Projects

- highlight key issues
- manage tasks
- discuss types of contract
- talk about the scope of a project

Kicking off

Speaking **1** Work in pairs. Tick the statements you agree with. Explain your reasons.

1 A project has a beginning and an end.
2 A project needs people.
3 A project is led by a project manager (PM).
4 A project always has a team.
5 A project is always for a client.

2 What are the key factors in any construction project?

Listening **3** ▶ 🎧 **20** Listen to a project manager (PM) briefing her new team at a kick-off meeting. What two documents does she mention?

4 What does each document do? Listen again and check your answers.

5 ▶ 🎧 **21** Listen to the next part of the briefing. The PM talks about three issues that affect each other. Write them in the chart.

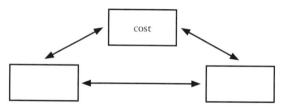

6 What does the PM say about her role in the project? Listen again and check your answer.

Vocabulary **7** Match the words in bold in 1–7 with their meanings a–g.

1 Have you seen the first draft
of the **project plan**?
2 The project manager clarified the
scope of the project at the meeting.
3 The new **WBS** software is saving us
a lot of time.
4 Rashid will be in charge of co-ordinating
resources for the project.
5 The accountants are not happy with
the **budget**.
6 The room for the **kick-off meeting**
has been changed. It's now in Room 2E.
7 The WBS splits the work into
smaller **elements**.

a) components
b) document summarising
all aspects of the project
c) Work Breakdown
Structure
d) cost breakdown
e) first meeting
f) the work that needs to
be done
g) people, materials and
other assets available
for the project

Speaking **8** Work in pairs. What other things happen at a kick-off meeting? Discuss.

Pronunciation: sentence stress	
Where you put the stress in a sentence changes the meaning of what you say.	*I just want to clarify some points about how I see <u>this</u> project running.* (not other projects) *I just want to clarify some points about how <u>I</u> see this project running.* (my perspective, not yours) *I just want to clarify some points about <u>how</u> I see this project running.* (the way I see it)

9 Read the sentences. Identify the word(s) you need to emphasise to mean a–c in each question.

1 First of all I want to stress the importance of the project plan.
   a) In a minute I will give you other points – this one is only the first. *First of all*
   b) not the other plans
   c) This is my personal perspective.

2 All of us need to be very familiar with this document.
   a) not another document
   b) not other people
   c) not just a little

3 It's important that you see the big picture, too.
   a) as well as the other points we have discussed
   b) the people in this room
   c) not just your own area of interest

10 ▶ 🎧 22 Listen and underline the emphasised word. Then, in pairs, discuss how the change in emphasis changes the meaning.

1 <u>We</u> need to get the roof finished before the rainy season starts.
2 We need to get the roof finished before the rainy season starts.
3 We need to get the roof finished before the rainy season starts.
4 We need to get the roof finished before the rainy season starts.
5 We need to get the roof finished before the rainy season starts.

Speaking 11 Work in pairs. Decide how these comments from project meetings relate to cost, time and/or scope. Explain your reasons.

1 We had so many meetings during the planning phase, just to discuss the WBS.
2 The timber we ordered is stuck in the port: the dockers are on strike. We can replace it, but it's going to cost about 50 percent more.
3 The deadline is the end of June. We're still on target.
4 I'm going to clear this invoice with the client – it's a bit more than we had originally forecast.
5 I'll send you a revised project plan. You'll get it by Friday.
6 Can you discuss these specifications with the architect after the visit? They don't look right to me.
7 They used the wrong additives in the concrete. It's already cracking.

12 Practise reading the sentences in 9 aloud, changing the emphasis to change the meaning.

Project meetings

Speaking **1** Use the words in the box to talk about the type of meetings you attend. Are any of them project meetings?

> length   location   participants   planned or impromptu   topic(s)

Listening **2** ▶ 🎧 23 Listen to part of a meeting and answer the questions.

1 What type of meeting is it?
2 What is the problem?

3 Listen again and answer these questions.

1 What are the reasons she gives for the problem?
2 Who has she spoken to about the problem?
3 How is she planning to solve the problem?

Speaking **4** This is a Gantt chart, which is often used to manage project tasks. How does it work? Discuss with a partner.

	MARCH				APRIL				MAY				JUNE			
Preparation of the ground	█															
Special foundations		█	█	█												
Adjustments of surface		█														
Infrastructure				█												
Roofs					█											
Bulk heading					█	█										
Interiors						█	█									
Treatment								█								
Grounds									█							
Ceilings										█						
Plumbing											█	█				
Electricity													█			

5 Think about your own situation. How do people communicate? Do you know any other tools which are used in projects?

Language

Present perfect	
We use the **present perfect** (have + past participle) to talk about things that happened in the past but not at a specific time.	*I **have discussed** this with the directors.* *We **have decided** to set up a portal.* *Why **haven't** you **actioned** the email?* *Who **has** he **spoken** to?*
Note that we often use **now, just** and **already** with the present perfect.	*I have **now/just/already** spoken to the client and we can go ahead.*

6 Make questions in the present perfect using these prompts.

1 you / speak to / the electricians?
2 he / write / the new WBS?
3 they / deliver / all the timber?
4 she / meet / the client?
5 you / hear / the weather forecast?
6 how many times / they / visit / the site?
7 why / they / not answer / the email?

7 Complete these responses.

1 Have you seen Mr Pavlak?   Yes, I've just _____ him.
2 Have you been to the site?   No, I _____ .
3 Has the supervisor arrived yet?   Yes, he _____ . He's in Building 13.
4 Why haven't you actioned the email?   Sorry. I've _____ too busy.
5 Has he finished?   Not yet. He's built the wall, but he _____ painted it.
6 Where's John?   He's _____ the keys again. He's looking for them.
7 Have you used the portal at all?   Yes, it's great. In fact, I've _____ entered the data.

8 Answer these questions. Compare your answers with a partner.

1 Have you already eaten today?
2 Have you just drunk a cup of coffee?
3 Have you ever visited other countries?
4 Have you ever used a Gantt Chart?
5 Have you ever taken part in project meetings? Give details.

Speaking **9** Work in pairs to roleplay a telephone call between a project manager and a member of the project team. Student A: Use the information below. Student B: Turn to page 68.

Student A: You are a member of a project team. You've lost your copy of the to-do list that the project manager gave you. The PM will go through the list and ask if you've completed the tasks. Answer 'no' to each task and give a different excuse each time.

No, I'm sorry, I haven't.
I've been too busy today.

Contracts

Speaking **1** What is a contract? Why are contracts important? Discuss with a partner.

Listening **2** ▶ **24** Listen to a consultant explaining three types of contract to a client. Circle the three types you hear.

> cost plus   fixed percentage   lump sum   renovation   turnkey

3 Match these descriptions to the three types of contract in 2. Then listen again and check your answers.

1 design and build   _____
2 fixed amount of money   _____
3 cost of materials and labour plus extra payment   _____

Vocabulary **4** Match the financial words 1–5 with their meanings a–e.

1 fixed fee   a) one payment
2 bonus   b) money not spent
3 lump sum   c) an extra amount of money
4 cost overrun   d) an agreed payment that does not change
5 savings   e) higher costs than originally forecast

Reading **5** Read these extracts about new projects. Match words to these meanings

1 an offer to carry out work for an agreed sum (Extract 1)
2 put a piece of equipment into service (Extract 2)
3 give or present something for approval (Extract 3)
4 the possibility (Extract 4)

1
After analysing the various tenders, the city authorities selected JEMMAG Construction to provide general contracting services for a new recreation centre in the Northfield district. The estimated construction cost is $23 million. 'This was not the lowest bid,' said a councillor, 'but we all felt it gave us the most attractive solution.'

2
Lakrah LLC has started planning for a new $145,000,000 project for the city energy utilities. 'Most companies in the area were not big enough to take on such a large project', said the mayor. 'Lakrah LLC will be responsible for all construction works as well as the delivery and commissioning of two gas turbines. We wanted to find someone who could simply do the whole job for a fixed fee.'

3
Most companies submitted bids which were far too high for the hospital's budget. In the end we awarded the contract to Kolbek and Partners, who will take over full responsibility for the project. The reasons for choosing Kolbek were not only financial; their design also made the most intelligent use of the existing facilities.

4
The city is looking for bidders to carry out a study which will examine the feasibility of widening the ring road between Junctions 45 and 49. The mayor is keen to find a solution which will avoid cost overruns. Opposition is expected from a number of groups due to the fact that the project will take place in one of our most important areas of natural beauty.

6 Find examples of the word *most* in the extracts in 5. Decide whether each example describes a noun or makes a comparison.

7 Complete these collocations with nouns from the extracts in 5.

1 award a _____
2 carry out a _____
3 examine the _____
4 take over _____
5 submit a _____
6 take on a _____
7 find a _____
8 analyse a _____
9 provide _____

8 Work in pairs. Add other nouns that go with the verbs in 7.

9 Read the collocations in 7 again. Have you ever done any of these things yourself? Discuss with a partner.

Language

Most	
Most can be used: to describe a noun. In this sense, **most** means **the majority of**.	most companies/most organisations/most people
Most can be used to make a comparison. In this sense **the most** means **the one that is more than any other**.	the most intelligent person/the most beautiful design/the most important issue

10 Complete these statements with *most* or *the most*. Do you agree with the statements?

1 _____ people in the construction industry have never been on a construction site.
2 In the UK _____ old buildings are listed.
3 The client is _____ important person in any project.
4 _____ building inspectors work for local authorities.
5 _____ engineers are not familiar with project management tools.
6 _____ unskilled labourers work on a temporary basis.
7 One of _____ difficult tasks in project management is avoiding cost overruns.

listed = term used in the UK to show an old building is protected by government order

11 Work in pairs. List the financial words from 4 and 5. Then use the words in a roleplay.

Student A: You are a potential client. Ask Student B (a building contractor) to clarify the meaning of some of the words on the list.
Student B: You are a building contractor. Explain the meaning of the words that Student A (a potential client) asks about.
A: *Could you explain the meaning of* **lump sum**, *please?*
B: *Yes, of course. Lump sum is when you …*
Then swap roles, find a new partner and repeat the roleplay.

12 Work in small groups. Describe types of contract that you are familiar with.

Focus on a project:
Wroclaw–Katowice Motorway, Poland

Speaking **1** Look at this illustration of the construction of a motorway toll area. Imagine you are in the project team that provides the things in the illustration. With a partner, brainstorm the scope of the project.

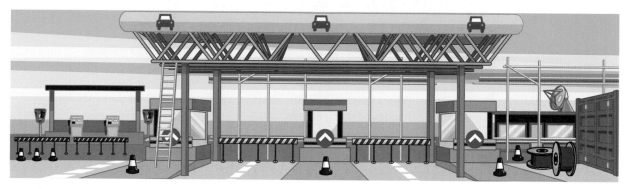

Reading **2** Read this text about construction work on the Wroclaw–Katowice Motorway in Poland. Decide which phrase best describes the overall scope of the project.

1 toll installation
2 transport equipment improvements
3 transport infrastructure upgrade
4 road buildings renovation
5 construction and maintenance overhaul

The A4 Wroclaw–Katowice toll motorway

EGSTRA, a consortium composed of Egis Projects and Strabag Sp z.o.o., were awarded the contract, worth €50 million, to upgrade the 162 km section of motorway between Wroclaw and Katowice. The contract consisted of designing, supplying and installing:

- 14 tolling stations with a total of 68 lanes and associated toll central computer
- 3 maintenance centres
- 162 road emergency phone boxes and associated call central computer
- 162 km of optic fibre with associated telecommunication equipment and network management system

- 2 traffic statistical stations, 1 Weight In Motion station and associated traffic central computer.

The contract covered two phases. The first phase, construction, was expected to last 24 months. The second phase was a maintenance period for all the equipment installed during the first phase, and was expected to last a further 36 months.

The client for the project was the Polish Road Directorate. As consortium leaders, Egis Projects were responsible for the design, supply, delivery, commissioning and maintaining of all fixed equipment. Strabag Sp z.o.o. were in charge of the buildings.

3 Identify what these numbers refer to in the text.

| 2 | 3 | 14 | 36 | 50 | 68 | 162 |

4 Answer these questions about the project.

1 Who is the client?
2 Who is the consortium leader?
3 Who is responsible for the construction of the buildings?
4 What is the value of the contract?
5 How long is construction expected to take?

Speaking **5** Work in pairs. Student A: Turn to page 69. Student B: Turn to page 68.

Review

Language **1** Complete this email with the present perfect form of the verbs in the box.

> agree   be   happen   have   increase   solve   start   work

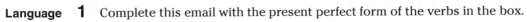

I just want to update you on what (1) _____ over the last few months.
As you know we (2) _____ now _____ phase two of the project
and the client (3) _____ to the changes we wanted. Tom and his team
(4) _____ very busy with all the different sub-contractors and we
(5) _____ the number of people in the logistics group. There are now twenty,
up from fifteen. I would now like to introduce Abdul Mohammed, who will be joining us
for this phase. He (6) _____ on many projects in this area and knows the
local conditions very well. We (7) _____ already _____ a couple
of very useful discussions about cement delivery, for example, and he
(8) _____ the rebar problem we had last week.

Vocabulary **2** Complete these sentences with the words in the box. There is one extra word.

> awarded   bids   client   fixed   savings   study   sum   tools

1   The contract was _____ to a contractor from New York.
2   He was asked to carry out a feasibility _____ for the client.
3   The city authorities have asked for _____ to be submitted by the
    end of the month.
4   They have agreed on a lump _____ for the work.
5   The client thinks we can make _____ if we use cheaper materials.
6   The most important person at the kick-off meeting was the _____ .
7   The new software includes a number of project management _____ .

Reading **3** Read the text about contracts and answer these questions.

1   What is the difference between the two models?
2   What are the advantages and disadvantages of the DB model?

> Traditionally, most companies use a design bid build (DBB) model.
> The client finds a company to design their project and then looks for
> a construction company (or companies) to build it for them. Different
> companies bid for the work. And finally, the contractor with the most
> attractive offer is selected and becomes responsible for the project. In
> the design build (DB) model, the client only has one point of contact.
> This may be an architect, for example, or a general contractor. There is
> no bidding. This means that the DB system is faster and cheaper, but of
> course the client has to hope that quality is not compromised. It is easy
> for a contractor to cut corners.

Documentation

- explain document control procedures
- talk about amendments
- give specific information abo[ut] documents
- discuss project documentatio[n]

Document control

Speaking **1** Work in pairs. Brainstorm types of document used in the construction industry.

Listening **2** ▶ 🔘 **25** A manager is showing a new employee around the company. Listen and note down at least three documents he mentions.

3 Listen again and answer these questions.

1 What is a document controller?
2 Why is document control necessary?
3 What is the difference between an RFI and an RFI log?
4 Why isn't the whole document control system computerised?
5 Why do some documents need to be archived?

Reading **4** Look at these three documents and decide what types of document they are. Choose from the names in the box.

> a change order procedure   a contract   an engineering drawing
> a job site memo   a report   an RFI log

A

To: All subcontractors
From: Roberto Camilleri
Memo 289 Traffic Control

Please note that with immediate effect all works traffic is to use Gate B to exit the site. This is to comply with local police requirements.

Roberto Camilleri
Project Manager
4 May

B

Request for information

Project: KL Building M (Foundations)
Project Manager: Roberto Camilleri

Number	Subject	Status	Date rec'd	Date completed
001	Broken pile	Proceed	3/11	
002	Pump oil	Closed	3/11	4/11
003	Pile orientation	Approved	3/11	4/11
004	Pier 23 Steel	Rejected	4/11	4/11

C

Emergency change orders require immediate action to avoid a serious work stoppage, delay and/or extra costs. Verbal approval may be given by the Project Manager, and is to be followed up in writing within one week (Form 34B). The approval is to include details of the emergency situation and, if possible, an estimate of the costs involved.

5 Complete this document control procedure with the words in the box.

amended   archived   books out   figures
log   number   scan   track   version

When a document comes in, we first make a handwritten note in the (1) _____ . If necessary, we give it a serial (2) _____ . We then (3) _____ it in, so that we have a permanent electronic record. As you can see, the serial number ends with a slash and then another number, always three (4) _____ . So, 001 is the first (5) _____ of the document. If the document is (6) _____ or updated in any way, it receives a new version number and so on. We also use the log to (7) _____ the movement of the document. If someone (8) _____ the document, the date and time are recorded here and when it comes back in, the date and time are recorded again. At the end of the project, the document is either destroyed or (9) _____ , depending on its importance.

Listening **6** ▶ 🔊 **26** Listen to a conversation about a document management system. Label the buttons on the screenshot.

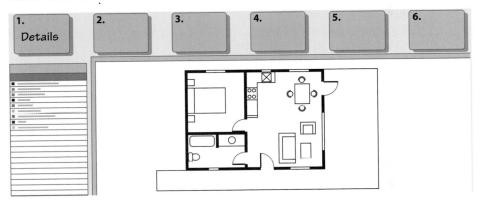

1. Details   2.   3.   4.   5.   6.

7 Listen again. What does the user see when he/she clicks each button?

Language

Have to

We use **have to** to show that we are required to do something.	We **have to** keep certain documents for three years. We **will have to** move to a fully computerised system. This **has to** be sent to all the subcontractors. The client had some new ideas, so we **had to** amend the floor plan.

8 Match 1–7 with a–g to make sentences.

1 We have to send the amendments
2 You have to press
3 We have to log and
4 We have to make sure that each document
5 I have to book every document in and
6 Key documents have to be
7 The name has to be

a) enter.
b) has a serial number.
c) first thing tomorrow.
d) out of the document centre.
e) track every document.
f) written in capital letters.
g) locked in the safe at night.

Speaking **9** Work in pairs. Design a simple log sheet for tracking documents. Explain how to use it. *You have to put the date in this column.*

Compare your log sheet with others in the class.

Amendments

1 Look at these extracts and decide what type of document they are from.

A

GENERAL NOTES

1. All dimensions in mm.
2. All load bearing walls to be minimum 200 mm thick.
3. Concrete mix ratios as follows:
   (i) structural concrete 1:1½:3 (cement: sand: aggregate)
   (ii) blinding concrete 1:3:5 (cement: sand: aggregate)
4. Concrete covers as follows:
   (i) substructures   50 mm
   (ii) columns   40 mm
   (iii) beams   35 mm
5. All structural steel to be painted with two coats of primer (one after fabrication and one after erection).
6. All plates to be mild steel to GS 5950;

B

SCHEDULE OF DRAWINGS

Drawing no.	Description	Sheet no.
GF/400/001	Site plan	1 of 1
GF/400/002	Floor plans	1–5 of 5
GF/400/013	Foundations – warehouse	1–4 of 4
GF/400/004	Warehouse elevations and section	1–6 of 6
GF/400/005	Wall details	1 of 1
GF/400/006	Plumbing diagrams	1–7 of 7

C

PLUMBING LEGEND	
SYMBOL	DESCRIPTION
⟠	POINT OF CONNECTION
– — CW – —	DOMESTIC COLD WATER, INSULATED
– -- – HW – -- –	DOMESTIC HOT WATER, INSULATED
—— SAN ——	NEW SANITARY SEWER
- - - - - V - - - - -	SANITARY VENT
▢	FLOOR DRAIN
C.A.	COMPRESSED AIR
Ⓜ〜R	WATER METER WITH REMOTE READER
—— G ——	GAS LINE

Listening **2** 🔊 27 Listen to the telephone conversation about the extracts in 1 and answer these questions.

1 What are the speakers' jobs?
2 What is the call about?

3 There are five changes to the extracts in 1. Listen again and mark the changes.

4 Circle the word on the right with the correct meaning of the word on the left in the context of the extracts in 1.

1 schedule   a project time plan / a list / to arrange (a meeting)
2 legend   a story / a table of symbols / a famous person
3 sheet   a piece of plastic used to cover things / a flat piece of metal / a large piece of paper

5 Complete this table with the missing nouns or verbs.

VERB	NOUN
abbreviate	
alter	
amend	
modify	*modification*
	revision

Language

Punctuation

.	full stop/period (but note that for numbers we say 'point 3' for .3)
/	slash/forward slash
,	comma
:	colon (but note that when we say ratios, we say '1 to 3', not '1 colon 3')
;	semi-colon
–	dash
()	brackets
" "	inverted commas
i, ii, iii, iv, etc.	Roman numerals
H	capital H
Note how we say:	
(ix)	'Roman numerals 9, in brackets', or 'Open brackets, Roman numerals 9, close brackets.'
'KZ'	'Capital K, capital Z, in inverted commas', or 'Open inverted commas, capital K capital Z, close inverted commas.'

6 Work in pairs. Student A: Use the information below. Student B: Turn to page 69.

Student A: Dictate this list to your partner.

1 Drg No. CD/356/001
2 (iv) concrete mix ratios 1:3:6
3 M–2 Unit 'A' and 'B' A/C plans
4 ISO/IEC 27001:2005
5 For .5/.25 ink system, 7 and 10 mm diameters apply

7 Test your partner. Draw some symbols used in construction drawings. Ask your partner what they mean. Then write a legend for any new symbols you find useful.

Specifying

Reading **1** Read this email and identify the piece of information that is missing.

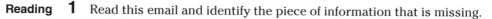

From: mman@psl.net
To: tenders@ministrypublicworks.gov

Project: KZH 897

This email is to notify you that it is our intention to bid for the above-mentioned project which was advertised on your website. Please send any information regarding the project to my office at this address.

Yours sincerely,

Mustafa Mohammed Al Najashi

Project Manager

Listening **2** **▶ 🎧 28** Listen to the telephone conversation about the bid. Identify the illustration that shows the project Mr Al Najashi is bidding for. What was the problem?

3 In the conversation two types of address are mentioned. What are they and what is the difference between them? Listen again and check your answers.

Reading **4** Read the email that Mr Al Najashi sent to Mr Campbell next. What is the situation now?

Dear Mr Campbell,

Thank you very much for the information pack which arrived this morning. My staff are already working on the bid and we plan to send you the completed forms tomorrow in time for the deadline.

Apologies again for the misunderstanding about the email address.

With best wishes,

Mustafa Mohammed Al Najashi

Project Manager

5 Read the two emails again and answer these questions.
1 Where was the project advertised?
2 When did the information pack arrive?

Listening **6** When did Mr Al Najashi send the first email? Listen again and check your answer.

Language

Relative clauses

We often use *which* or *that* to give specific information about the thing we are talking about.	*It is our intention to bid for the project* **which/that** *was advertised on your website.* *Thank you for the information pack* **which/that** *arrived this morning.* *Is it your company* **which/that** *is doing the bridge refurbishment on the same highway?*
We can leave out *which* if it is followed by a pronoun.	*It's about an email (***which/that***) I sent you on 27 May.* *Have you looked at the draft (***which/that***) I wrote this morning?*

7 Match 1–7 to a–g to make sentences.

1	Here's the letter which you	a)	on his desk.
2	The document that you	b)	need is with the client.
3	We are still looking for the drawings which	c)	wrote this morning?
4	The letter which I sent you yesterday	d)	revised.
5	Where is the contract that I signed	e)	was not the final draft.
6	Have you looked at the draft which I	f)	last week?
7	Here are the documents that we found	g)	you redrafted.

8 Read these sentences. Use brackets to show where we can leave out *which* or *that*.

1 The manual which I sent you has not come back.
2 He needs to rewrite the letter that he drafted yesterday.
3 We discussed the specifications which we received last week.
4 Where is the change order that was sent this morning?
5 The email which I sent last week was ignored.
6 I'm looking for the RFI log that was on the desk.
7 The documents which are kept in the safe are all confidential.
8 Where's the drawing which contains the details of the retaining wall?
9 Have they sent us the change order which we asked for?

Speaking **9** Work in pairs. Take turns to choose a document type from the first box. Tell your partner exactly which document you need. Use words from the second box to be more specific. Follow the example conversation below.

agenda	change order	contract	drawing	email	floor plan	manual
minutes	permit	presentation	procedure	report	RFI log	schedule

amended	archived	backed up	destroyed	redrafted	revised
	signed	wrote			

A: I need a copy of the contract.
B: Which contract?
A: The contract which we signed last week.
B: We signed two contracts last week.
A: I need the one which has to do with the residential housing project in Takara Road.
B: OK.

Focus on a project: Golf course construction

Reading **1** Castle Golf is an American company which designs and builds miniature golf courses. Read Castle Golf's design and build process and underline the document types it mentions.

The Castle Golf Design and Build Process

1 Castle Golf and client begin conversation. Castle Golf sends literature and emails helpful information. Questions are answered, project goals are discussed and clarifications occur as we seek a high level of comfort.

2 Client decides to use Castle Golf.

3 Client and Castle Golf enter into a retainer/design agreement, the fee based on the magnitude of the project.

4 Client and Castle Golf explore target customers and appropriate styles including theme, hole designs, etc. Client may send photos, postcards, etc.; sometimes the client has a Castle Golf representative visit the site.

5 Client sends site plans, topography and other required information to allow the design work to proceed.

6 Castle Golf begins development of layout and preliminary plan.

7 Client and Castle Golf review initial plan before progressing further. This is a concept procedure to see if we are on the right track.

8 A final design layout ready for pricing will be attained and then the process of design and budget reconciliation typically occurs.

9 Upon arriving at an agreement on design and cost, Castle Golf will prepare a construction contract for client review, approval and deposit.

10 Castle Golf develops construction documents and arrives on site to begin construction of the project.

11 While Castle Golf is constructing the project, the agreed-upon theme structures, props and effects will be fabricated and delivered to the site for installation.

12 Construction is completed and play begins.

2 Categorise the types of document from the text.

DESIGN DOCUMENTS	CONTRACTUAL DOCUMENTS	CONSTRUCTION DOCUMENTS
literature and emails		

Speaking **3** Work in pairs. Imagine you are document controllers. Decide which categories in 2 are the most important to control. Explain how you would log and track them.

Review

1 Find words in the box which are similar in meaning to the words in **bold**.

> amend   bid   contract   draft   electronic   minutes   private

1 Can you send us the documents in **digital** format, please?
2 We need to lock these drawings away – they're **confidential**.
3 Have you had a chance to **revise** the legend yet?
4 The **tender** documents need to go in by next Friday.
5 Don't worry, all the details are in the written **agreement**.
6 This is the first **version** of the letter – have you seen the latest one?
7 I would like to see the **record** of the meeting.

2 Match 1–6 with a–f.

1 handwritten   a) number
2 site   b) plan
3 change   c) order
4 submission   d) changes
5 minor   e) note
6 serial   f) date

3 Complete these conversations with *have to*, *has to* or *had to*.

1 A: What's the problem with the safe?
  B: I've lost the combination. I'll _____ call the locksmith now. What a hassle.
2 A: What's the hurry?
  B: I need to find Alima. I've just heard she _____ apply for the permits by next Monday.
3 A: Where were you this morning?
  B: In Samir's office. We _____ sign the contract.
4 A: Why are the lights on in the office? It's after seven.
  B: The document controllers are working late. They _____ scan in the paperwork which arrived this afternoon so we can use it tomorrow.
5 A: Do you know where Pedro is?
  B: He _____ go to the printer's to pick up the drawings.

4 Name the punctuation.

1 .   _____
2 ,   _____
3 ;   _____
4 ( ) _____
5 /   _____
6 –   _____
7 ' ' _____
8 ii _____

5 Insert *which* or *that*, if necessary.

1 The letter I sent yesterday has come back: 'not known at this address'.
2 Have you seen the change order arrived yesterday?
3 I need a copy of the presentation you gave yesterday.
4 Where is the copy of the contract I asked for?
5 He wants us to look at the drawings are in the archives.

8

Health and safety

- communicate health and safety guidelines
- give instructions for traffic contro
- describe incidents
- discuss hurricane precautions

Health and safety guidelines

Speaking **1** Look at the final slide from a health and safety presentation. With a partner, decide what topics are in the presentation.

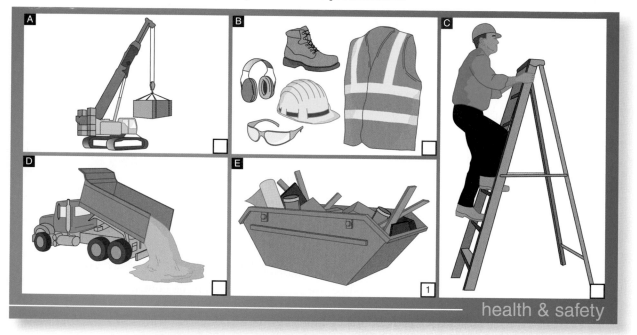

Listening **2** [🔊 29] Listen to the presentation. Number the illustrations in 1 in the order the speaker mentions them.

3 Match 1–5 with a–e. Then listen again to check.

1 What did the speaker say about hazardous waste?
2 What is one of the most common accidents?
3 What did he say about rigging loads?
4 What happened in sand last year?
5 What did he call protective clothing?

a) He said, 'Waste needs to be sorted properly and dealt with properly.'
b) He called it PPE.
c) He told us not to rig loads unless we're trained to do it.
d) He said it's falls.
e) He said that one person died by being buried alive.

Vocabulary **4** Choose the correct verb to complete the advice.

1 *Follow / Take / Name* the instructions.
2 *Take / Give / Receive* proper precautions.
3 *Don't fall / Don't cut / Don't rig* corners.
4 *Take / Break / Remember* your time.
5 *Take / Use / Keep* the equipment.
6 *Keep / Handle / Wear* your hard hat.
7 *Use / Follow / Keep* the recommendations.

Language

Reporting instructions and advice

There are different ways to report instructions and advice. One way is to say exactly the same thing.	He **said**, 'Don't cut corners.' He **said**, 'Keep your eyes open.'
Another way is to use **told**. (Note that **told** needs an object.)	He **told us** not to cut corners. He **told us** to keep our eyes open.
Note that like **say** and **tell**, some verbs need an object and some do not.	He **recommended that** we … He **warned us** not to … He **instructed us** to … He **suggested that** we …

5 Complete these conversations with *say, said, tell* or *told*.

1 A: Put the cone over there.
   B: What did he _____ ?
   C: He _____ , 'Put the cone over there.'
   B: Next to the other cone?
   C: Yes, that's right.

2 A: Put out the road works sign.
   B: What did he _____ me to do?
   C: He _____ you to put out the road works sign.
   B: Where do I get a road works sign from?
   C: I don't know. Go and ask him. He _____ us to ask him if we had any questions.

3 A: Pick up the debris and put it in the skip.
   B: What did she _____ ?
   C: She _____ , 'Pick up the debris and put it in the skip.'
   B: Why?
   C: I don't know. Just do as you're _____ .

4 A: Get Tony to check the rigging.
   B: What did he _____ ?
   C: He _____ us to get Tony to check the rigging.
   B: Sorry. What did you _____ ?
   C: I _____ that he _____ us to get Tony to check the rigging.
   B: OK, OK, no need to shout!

Speaking **6** Work in pairs. Read the advice and report it to your partner. Student A: Use the information below. Student B: Turn to page 69 and follow the instructions.

Student A: You're an apprentice painter. Read the advice from your supervisor about using electrical equipment. Report it to your partner.

> Keep wet hands away from electrical equipment and light switches.
> Don't disconnect anything by pulling on the cable. Pull out the plug.
> Unplug equipment when it isn't in use.
> Don't cover switches with wallpaper paste.

He told us to keep wet hands away from …

7 Write some advice for a piece of equipment that you are familiar with. Then share the advice with others in the class.

Traffic control

1 Look at the illustration from the UK Department for Transport road safety guidelines. Label it with the words in the box.

> barrier   'end of road works' sign   hazard   'keep right' sign   kerb   lane
> 'road narrows ahead' sign   'road works' sign   single carriageway
> traffic cone   vehicle

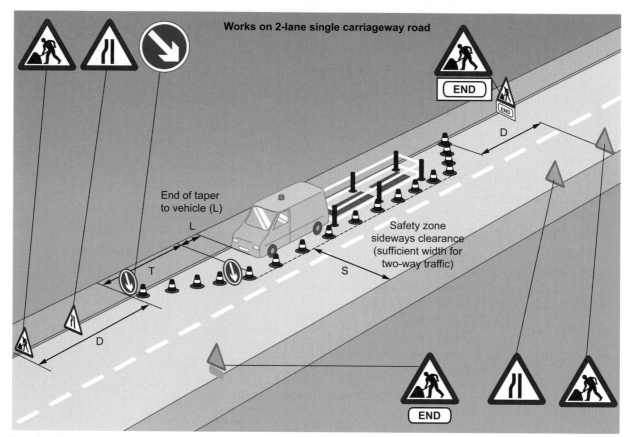

Works on 2-lane single carriageway road

End of taper to vehicle (L)

Safety zone sideways clearance (sufficient width for two-way traffic)

Reproduced from the Department of Transport website: http://www.dft.gov.uk

Listening **2** ▶ 🎧 30 Listen to a site supervisor giving instructions about setting out the site in 1. What is the supervisor's role?

3 Listen again. How long are D and T in the illustration in 1?

Vocabulary **4** Work in pairs. Discuss the meaning of these phrases.
1 oncoming traffic
2 face the traffic
3 volume of traffic

a taper

5 Look at this table. Calculate the speed limit of the road in 1. Is the supervisor correct when he says he needs five metres between the cones?

Safety at street works and road works
Size and siting distance: details of signs and cones and safety zone dimensions

Type of road	Minimum and normal maximum sitting distance (D) of first sign in advance of lead-in taper (metres)	Minimum clear visibility to first sign (metres)	Minimum size of signs (mm)	Minimum height of signs (mm)	Sideways Safety Zone (S)	Details of lead-in cone tapers Recommended lengths	1	2	3	4	5	6	7
Single carriageway road, restricted to 30 mph or less	20 to 45	60	600	450	0.5 m	Length of taper (T) in metres	13	26	39	52	65	78	91
						Minimum No. of cones	4	4	6	7	9	10	12
						Minimum No. of lamps at night	3	3	5	6	8	9	11
Single carriageway road, restricted to speeds of 31 to 40 mph inclusive	45 to 110	60	750	450	0.5 m	Length of taper (T) in metres	20	40	60	80	100	120	140
						Minimum No. of cones	4	6	8	10	13	15	17
						Minimum No. of lamps at night	3	5	7	9	12	14	16
All purpose dual carriageway road, restricted to 40 mph or less	110 to 275	60	750	450	0.5 m	Length of taper (T) in metres	25	50	75	100	125	150	175
						Minimum No. of cones	4	7	10	13	15	18	21
						Minimum No. of lamps at night	3	6	9	12	14	17	20
Single carriageway road, with speed limit of 50 mph or more	275 to 450	75	750	450	1.2 m	Length of taper (T) in metres	25	50	75	100	125	150	175
						Minimum No. of cones	4	7	10	13	15	18	21
						Minimum No. of lamps at night	3	6	9	12	14	17	20
All purpose dual carriageway road, with speed limit of 50 mph or more	725 to 1600	105	1200	750	1.2 m	Length of taper (T) in metres	32	64	96	128	160	192	224
						Minimum No. of cones	5	9	12	16	19	23	26
						Minimum No. of lamps at night	4	8	11	15	18	22	25

Speed limit (mph)	30 or less	40	50	60	70
Minimum longways clearance (L) metres	½	15	30	60	100

Reproduced from the Department of Transport website: http://www.dft.gov.uk

6 Use the illustration in 1 and the tables in 5 to complete this table.

	D	T	S	L
1 Hazard width 3 metres; Single carriageway; 50 mph speed limit	275–450m	75m	1.2m	30m
2 Hazard width 2 metres; Dual carriageway; 30 mph speed limit				
3 Hazard width 5 metres; Dual carriageway; 50 mph speed limit				

Giving instructions

In spoken English we can use **need** to give instructions.	We **need** more width./This **needs** to be wider. The spacing between the cones **needs** to be increased/bigger. This **needs** to be 12 metres long and 3 metres wide. The sideways/longways clearance **needs** to be at least … We **need** at least 12 metres clearance here.

7 Work in pairs. Discuss how to set out a site if the works are in the centre of the road. Draw a sketch.

8 What do you know about traffic control and site safety regulations in your country?

Incidents

Speaking **1** Many people get injured on construction sites every year. With a partner, brainstorm some common injuries.

Listening **2** ▶ 🎧 31 Listen to six conversations about accidents. Match these illustrations with the conversations.

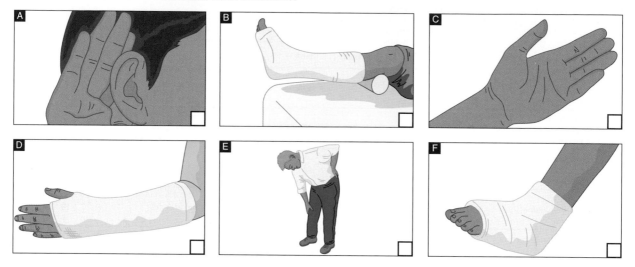

3 Complete these conversations with the words in the box. Listen again to check.

| back | ear | finger | foot | hands | knee | wrist |

white finger syndrome = also known as Hand Arm Vibration Syndrome (HAVS)

1 A: A friend of mine had white _____ syndrome from using vibrating power tools. He lost all feeling in his _____ .
   B: Sounds painful.

2 A: I had an accident last year. I tripped over a cable and fell. I put out my arm to stop myself and broke my _____ .
   B: Ouch. I bet that hurt.

3 A: I saw an accident this morning. One of the labourers dropped a load of bricks on his _____ . He was only wearing sandals, not safety boots, which didn't help.
   B: What? I'll speak to the manager. Everyone needs boots.

4 A: _____ injuries are very common. People lift things which are too heavy.
   B: Straight back, bend the knees. That's what I always say.

5 A: One of the drivers was hit by a truck. He wasn't wearing his hi-vis vest and the other driver didn't see him. The bumper hit his leg just below his _____ and fractured it.
   B: I bet he wears his vest from now on.

6 A: People don't use _____ protection and then damage their hearing. It's a gradual process, so they're not aware of what's happening.
   B: Pardon? What did you say?

Vocabulary   **4**   Read the conversations in 3 again. Underline the PPE (Personal Protective Equipment) items.

Speaking   **5**   Work in pairs. Discuss the precautions you need to take to prevent the injuries in 3.

Language

Past simple and past continuous	
We use the **past simple** to report what happened.	I **tripped** over a cable. I **broke** my wrist. The driver **didn't see** him.
We use the **past continuous** to describe an action in progress.	He **was wearing** sandals. He **wasn't wearing** his vest.
Past simple and past continuous	I **was talking** to the site manager when the fire **started**. He **was waiting** for the lumber delivery when the accident **happened**.

6   Complete these sentences with the correct past form of the verbs in brackets.

1. We were thinking about going home when the cement _____ . (arrive)
2. We _____ the column when the telephone rang. (pour)
3. I was having a cup of tea when I _____ that the winch was on fire. (notice)
4. She _____ the newspaper when the client came through the gate. (read)
5. He _____ the scaffolding when it suddenly _____ . (climb; collapse)

7   Match conversations 1–7 with a–g. Underline the examples of the past simple and past continuous.

1. Where did you go yesterday?
2. Where were they working yesterday?
3. What did you do last week?
4. How did he burn his hand?
5. What was she doing on site?
6. What happened?
7. When did the accident happen?

a) He was lifting a load when one of the slings snapped.
b) I went to the hospital. I had to see the doctor.
c) Just before our lunch break.
d) They were working on the bridge refurbishment on the other site.
e) She was visiting the apprentices.
f) I had a busy week. I worked on the new site plans.
g) He was working with the welders. He forgot the metal was hot.

Speaking   **8**   Work in pairs. Take turns to ask about an injury and explain how it happened.

A: *How did you break your arm?*
B: *I was walking along the road when I tripped over some debris.*
A: *Debris? What debris?*
B: *The skip was overflowing. There was debris everywhere.*

Focus on a project:
Hurricane preparations, Florida, USA

Speaking   **1**   Imagine you work on a construction site and receive a warning of bad weather: high winds and possible flooding. Work in pairs and list the preparations you need to make.

Reading   **2**   Hurricanes are common in Florida, USA. The Florida Home Builders Association gives hurricane preparation tips to construction sites. Read this extract from their guidelines and add to or change your list in 1.

Hurricane preparation tips for construction sites

Local emergency operations officials and the National Weather Service will provide hurricane landfall probabilities. Approximately 60 to 48 hours before the hurricane is expected to make landfall, consider cancelling the delivery of building materials to all job sites except any materials needed to secure the building site from storm damage.

While contractors generally don't want to stop or delay construction activities, the 48- to 24-hour window before landfall is the suggested time to stop all construction activity. It's important to note that most local building departments generally stop field inspections, except for those related to pouring columns, tie beams, wet decks, floors and similar structural items, during this time as well.

Contractors are encouraged to activate their hurricane job site plan during this window of time. Notify subcontractors to help secure the building site. Helpful hints for site protection include:

- Secure all job sites, giving priority attention to those located in the most populated areas.
- Clean up all construction debris.
- Tie or band together all loose plywood and lumber. Secure other loose building supplies.
- Remove permit board and all job site signage.
- Locate and turn off electricity, water and gas.

Also, secure all portable toilets. Portable toilets can also be anchored adjacent to L-shaped walls of the home under construction and they can be weighted down with concrete blocks or sand.

After the site is secure, advise subcontractors to leave and not return until the hurricane threat has passed. Make sure to have contact numbers for all subcontractors stored in a secure and dry place and that they know who will contact them after the hurricane passes.

Speaking   **3**   Work in small groups. One of you is a site manager and the others are subcontractors on a construction site near you.

Site manager: You have just received a hurricane warning. Make notes on the preparations you need to make. Then brief your subcontractors. Start like this:
There are a lot of preparations we need to make. First, we need to …
Subcontractors: You have just received a hurricane warning. The site manager will brief you on hurricane preparations. Make notes on the questions you need to ask. Then ask him/her the questions.
When do you want us to …? What about the …?

     4   Work with people from other groups. Compare your hurricane preparations.

He said, 'We need to remove all signage.'
She told us to check the batteries in our mobile phones.

Review

Vocabulary **1** Match the expressions in columns 1 and 2. Then match them to their definitions in column 3.

1 dual	a) zone	i) two lanes
2 length of	b) taper	ii) how fast you are allowed to drive
3 safety	c) traffic	iii) the smallest amount
4 traffic	d) carriageway	iv) how long the slant is on the row of traffic cones
5 oncoming	e) number	v) the cars coming towards you
6 speed	f) limit	vi) an area free of traffic where people can work
7 minimum	g) cone	vii) a piece of equipment used to control moving cars

Language **2** Read the supervisor's instructions. Then complete the labourer's summary with *told* or *said*. Correct the four errors in the labourer's summary.

Supervisor's instructions:
Listen carefully. Here's what I want you to do. First, fix the signs properly. Use sandbags to prevent them falling over. Second, make sure the signs are at least 150 metres away from the ditch. We need to give drivers enough warning. Third, keep checking the signs to make sure they haven't been knocked over by traffic.

Labourer's summary:
He (1) _____ us lots of things. First of all, he (2) _____ that he wants us to use cement to stop the signs falling over. Second, he (3) _____ we need to put the signs at least 15 metres away from the kerb. And third, he (4) _____ us to keep checking the signs to make sure they're not dirty.

3 Complete these sentences with your own ideas. Sometimes more than one word is possible.

1 I was walking along the road and I tripped over a _____ . I broke my _____ .
2 He was rigging the _____ when one of the _____ snapped. Luckily no one was hurt.
3 She was _____ to the supervisor when the _____ crashed into the barrier.
4 He was putting out the signs when a car _____ .
5 The hurricane started at about 6 p.m. The first thing that flew into the air was the _____ .

4 List the bad weather preparations for a construction site near you. Use the words in the box to help you.

| advise call cancel deliveries lumber portable toilet |
| secure signage subcontractors tie turn off |

Writing **5** Look at these illustrations and write the story about what happened to the construction worker.

Partner files

Student B

3 Equipment

Faults **Speaking exercise 8 page 23**

Student B: Use all the words in the box. Make up your own explanation as to what happened to the pipe.

> broken   leaking   pipe   road   tyre marks   unprotected

4 Materials

Focus on a project **Speaking exercise 4 page 34**

Student B: Look at this illustration of a crash barrier. Your partner has a different picture. Explain the construction (including layout and materials) to your partner, and then draw a sketch of your partner's construction. Discuss which construction is better for a race track like the BIC.

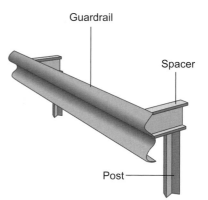

6 Projects

Project meetings **Speaking exercise 9 page 47**

Student B: You are the project manager. You gave your team member a to-do list. Phone him/her to check that the tasks have been completed. Note down the responses. Start like this:

Have you written a letter to the clients yet to explain the delays in the project?

To do:
- write letter to client (explaining the delays)
- organise delivery of new window frames to site
- print out project documentation
- order new software
- look at the new WBS
- update Gantt chart

Focus on a project **Speaking exercise 5 page 50**

Student B: Prepare a short talk about the companies involved in the Wroclaw-Katowice motorway project. Explain what companies are involved and what their responsibilities are. Be prepared to answer your partner's questions.

Alternatively, talk about the companies in a project you know about.

7 Documentation

Amendments **Speaking exercise 6 page 55**

Student B: Dictate this list to your partner.
1 Scale 1:50
2 Job No: ZH/362–06
3 Section IV,
  Part B – Schedule of drawings
4 Version: 1.0
  Date: 04/27/09
  Page 1 of 5
5 Pencil: Recommended H/2H or use HB

8 Health and safety

**Health and
safety guidelines** **Speaking exercise 6 page 61**

Student B: You're a labourer. Read the advice from your supervisor about working with or near heavy earth-moving equipment. Report it to your partner.

> Don't give hand signals unless you're trained.
> Make sure the driver can see you. Don't stand behind the vehicle.
> Keep away from cables and moving parts.
> Don't touch any controls or switches.

He told us not to give hand signals unless …

* *

Student A

4 Materials

Focus on a project **Speaking exercise 4 page 34**

Student A: Look at this illustration of a crash barrier. Your partner has a different picture. Explain the construction (including layout and materials) to your partner, and then draw a sketch of your partner's construction. Discuss which construction is better for a race track like the BIC.

Concrete retaining wall
Conveyor belt
1.1 m
Six tyres high
Bolted joints
Polypropylene tubes (approx 10mm wall)

6 Projects

Focus on a project **Speaking exercise 5 page 50**

Student A: Prepare a short talk about the scope of the Wroclaw-Katowice motorway project. Explain exactly what work needs to be done and in what order. Be prepared to answer your partner's questions.

Alternatively, talk about the scope of a construction project you know about.

Audio script

Unit 1 Teamwork

▶ 💿 2

[M = Martin   S = Sandra   A = Ahmed]

M: So ... how can I help you?

S: Well, we'd like some background information about the project ...

M: OK, I can ask my assistant to send you some details. We sent out a press release a couple of weeks ago.

S: Yes, we have a copy of that, thank you. We're interested in finding out more information about the people working here. How many workers do you have on site? What do they do? Where are they from? Are they all local people?

M: Oh, that depends on what's happening. As you can imagine, this is quite a complex business, so we have different subcontractors and suppliers coming in and out all the time.

S: OK.

M: But, to answer your question, I'd say we usually have about 100 people on site. And they're mostly from this area.

A: And you're in charge of the site?

M: Well, yes, my company – actually, my father's company – is the general contractor for the project. We co-ordinate all the subcontractors and make sure things stay on schedule and stay within budget. I report to the project manager, Sabina Tom.

A: I see. And your father is Kasper Karp?

M: Yes, that's right. Sometimes, on bigger projects, we work in a consortium with other contractors and companies.

S: Could you tell us something about ...?

M: Excuse me, I've just seen Mr Lang. He's walking through the gate. He represents the client, and I have a meeting with him and Anna Black in a few minutes' time ...

S: Anna Black?

M: Anna works for the cement supplier, DKI Cement. They're supplying all the cement for the project. Just a moment, please. My assistant, Robert Lane, will answer any further questions you have.

S and A: Thank you.

▶ 💿 3

1 My role is to make sure that all the project managers have the support they need for materials and equipment. We have a fleet of vehicles which the project managers and site managers use, and I also liaise with many different suppliers.

2 There are only five people in my department, two lawyers and three assistants. We handle all the contracts and claims.

3 My department works with all the other departments. The project managers work for me, but the people in the project teams come from the other departments. These teams change as the project goes through different phases.

4 Our main role is to work with the clients and our management to plan the projects and work out costs. We also help to look for new clients.

5 Our main task is to look after all the income and outgoings in the company. So we send out the bills to our clients and pay the suppliers.

6 We are the technical department. We do the maths and make sure that things work the way they should. We work a lot with Operations and also Business Development.

7 We help to recruit new staff and deal with training and development. We are also responsible for paying expenses and paying wages and salaries.

▶ 💿 4

1 A: So, let me go over some general points.

B: OK.

A: So, we start work every morning between seven and nine. You must be in by nine, OK?

B: Yes, that's fine.

A: Now then ... Your office is being renovated, so for the first couple of weeks you'll be in the site managers' office. They have a spare desk. You'll be able to move in to your office with the other engineers at the beginning of April. It's open-plan and very nice. There are new desks, new computers, ... even new plants.

B: Great. Any idea what CAD software we use?

A: No, sorry. You'll have to ask Jozef. He's responsible for IT. He'll give you your password, make sure you have all the right software, that sort of thing.

B: OK. It's very different to university.

A: Yes, I'm sure it is. OK. I think that's about it. Any other questions?

B: Yes, could you tell me about parking? Do I need a pass or anything?

A: Yes, yes, you do. Speak to Roza. She'll fix that for you.

B: OK, thank you.

2 A: Let's see. I normally work around 40 hours a week.

B: What time do you start work?

A: Every day is different. It depends on what's happening on the site. There's quite a lot of overtime, especially in the summer.

B: How did you get into this job?

A: I started as a clerk in an office. I didn't like that. I wanted an outdoor job. So when I was twenty, I got a job as a labourer on construction sites. After a year I got onto an apprenticeship programme. That took three years. I was sponsored by a local contractor. I spent twenty years working on large projects like hospitals, schools and factories. It's a hard physical job. I also have to bend a lot and lift things. And I spend a lot of time on my knees. I usually wear kneepads to protect my knees. A lot of the work is outside, so bad weather sometimes stops us working.

B: Where do you work now?

A: I'm self-employed now. I have two assistants and we do small jobs like driveways, pavements, that kind of thing.

3 A: I really do three things in my job. I measure dimensions of buildings. I work out where boundaries are, in other words where one property ends and another begins. And I look at the land and record details of topographic features like hills and slopes. I have an office, but I spend most of my time outdoors.

B: Do you use any special equipment?

A: I use GPS, which tells me my exact location. And of course I use a total station. I often use GIS applications, which help me analyse my data.

B: Sorry, what's GIS?

A: GIS stands for Geographic Information Systems.

A: How did you get into this job?

B: I was good at maths at school, especially algebra and trigonometry. I liked computers and software. And I wanted a job outdoors. I had a summer job on a construction site when I was a teenager, and I looked at all the different jobs. This one looked good.

Unit 2 Design

▶ 🎧 5

Right, so let's look at the floor plan. As you can see, the house is 28 foot long and 20 foot wide. This gives a total area of 560 square feet. The main room, with the kitchen, is 16 by 20 foot. The bedroom is 12 by 14 foot. And the bathroom is 6 by 14 foot. Note that all these dimensions are within a tolerance of plus or minus one inch. The rooms are standard height, 8 feet. The doors are all the same – 2 foot 8, or 32 inches wide, and 6 foot 8 high, not including the frames. Please note that these drawings are not to scale, so the dimensions are for guidance only.

▶ 🎧 6

First we look at various documents, such as preliminary specifications, drawings, utility requirements and so on – anything which can give us relevant information. We then calculate our initial estimate. As the design moves on into specific details – for example, floor plans, fittings, – we get more accurate. This means we include cost of labour, materials and plant, subcontractor quotes, and overheads – that's things like legal fees, building permits, on site temporary construction, transport and so on. We even allow for stoppages due to weather. For example, if it snows, we can't work on roofs. And then we add the profit we expect. Finally, we produce an estimate that can be sent to you, the client. This is the bid price.

▶ 🎧 7

[A = Fareed Ali   B = Giovanni Martini]

A: Fareed Ali.

B: Martini Pools, Giovanni Martini speaking. You sent us an email?

A: Ah, yes, Mr Martini. I'd like to build a swimming pool, an outdoor pool, in my garden here in Cairo. How much will it cost?

B: Can I just ask you a couple of questions? First of all, what size of swimming pool would you like?

A: About 20 by 10.

B: Is that metres?

A: Yes.

B: So ... a rectangle? No curves?

A: Yes, exactly.

B: And what about depth?

A: Say, two metres at the deep end and then a slope to the shallow end, with three steps at the shallow end.

B: No problem. Have you thought about the type of swimming pool? Gunite, which is very long lasting, is more expensive than, say, fibreglass or vinyl. Or maybe you want an above-ground pool?

A: What's gunite?

B: A type of concrete.

A: OK, yes, that sounds great.

B: OK, you'll also need to think about tiles and coping. Coping is what we have on the edge of the pool. There are a lot of options: stone, poured concrete, precast concrete, tiles, …

A: Of course.

B: Well, the price will depend on which you choose. And then there are things like plumbing and electrical equipment to install.

A: Can you explain?

B: Well, you'll need to think about pumps and filtration systems and so on.

A: I see.

B: Can you tell me something about the location? Excavation costs depend on the type of ground.

A: We're on the edge of the city. There is desert behind us. So it's mostly stone and sand with one or two trees to remove.

B: OK. Is it flat?

A: No, we're on a hill.

B: OK.

A: One last question. How long will it take?

B: Around two to three months, once we have a building permit. Again it depends on exactly what you want.

A: Yes, I understand.

B: OK, well, I have an idea of what you'd like now, but I need to see the site and discuss a few more details with you. Can I visit some time?

A: Can't you just send me an estimate?

B: Well, not really. To do this I need to have more information. I can only give you a very rough estimate. Very rough.

A: That's OK. So … how much?

B: Can I call you back in ten minutes? I need to do some calculations.

A: Yes, that's fine. Thank you. Goodbye.

B: Bye.

▶ 🔘 8

[A = Magda   B = Habib]

A: We need to make some modifications to the original plans.

B: What? Why?

A: The new client. He wants us to make some changes.

B: OK. So tell me … what changes?

A: Well, first he wants to build a floor-to-ceiling aquarium here, on the right. That means strengthening the floor.

B: OK. How about if I do some calculations and get back to you on that?

A: Yes, I'm OK with that. Thank you. Now, the lighting …

B: What about the lighting?

A: He wants more natural lighting. Do you have any thoughts?

B: I know, why don't we remove these dividing walls?

A: Yes, good idea. He also wants more space, a more open-plan design, so that fits in nicely. What do you think?

B: Well, they are only partition walls. But we'll need to run the workstation cabling through the floor. Maybe we need to raise the floor?

A: Yes, that's a good point. I'll speak to him again about this. Next thing … He wants better insulation. He thinks it's too noisy. Can you speak to Ahmed about that?

B: Sure.

A: OK, now the joinery.

B: What about the joinery?

A: Well, the doors and windows stay the same, but he wants us to use FSC timber. It's more environmentally friendly.

B: OK. How about if I speak to the joiners and see what they recommend?

A: OK. And we need to change the paint.

B: What about the paint?

A: He wants us to use natural paints. No VOCs.

B: Yes, that makes sense. But isn't that more expensive?

A: Yes, he knows. He's OK with that.

B: OK. I'll organise that.

A: And finally the air conditioning. He wants us to think about different systems, systems that are more energy-efficient if possible.

B: OK. I'll speak to the HVAC people.

A: There's no need. I'm seeing them later today. I'll speak to them.

B: Thank you.

Unit 3 Equipment

▶ 💿 9

1   This machine is for driving piles into the soil.
2   This machine has a bucket which is used to scoop soil out of the ground.
3   This machine can lift heavy loads high in the air.
4   You use this machine to move large amounts of earth.
5   This machine makes electricity from petrol.
6   This machine is used for transporting concrete to high parts of a construction site.
7   This machine is used to transport people to high parts of a construction site.

▶ 💿 10

A: Hi, Karl. You asked about the backhoe. A couple of things. One of the mirrors is cracked.
B: I thought it got fixed. Can you put it on the checklist?
A: Yes, I've already done that. And one of the belts was loose. I tightened it.
B: OK. Let's keep an eye on that. Anything else?
A: Well, the first aid kit is missing … and the fire extinguisher, too.
B: What, again? That's the third time this month! I'll speak to the security people.
A: And there's a problem with the hydraulics. Can you come and have a look?
B: Oh? What's up?
A: Look at this.
B: Yes, that's too much oil. Did you check the reservoir?
A: Yes, it's nearly empty.
B: OK. Let's have a look … Got a torch handy?
A: Yes, just a second … Here you are.
B: Ah, I see the problem.
A: What is it?
B: The hose is damaged here. Just behind the tank. Can you see?
A: Yes, I missed that, sorry. Shall I call Mohammed, then?
B: No, Mohammed's off sick today. But Farid should be around somewhere.
A: OK. I'll give him a call.
B: Tell Farid it's urgent. We need the backhoe to dig those trenches.
A: Yes, OK. I'm on it now.

▶ 💿 11

[A = Supervisor   B = John   C = Sandra]

A: OK, listen up. We need to sort out the office trailer. It's a bit of a mess. Here's what I want you to do. First of all, the roof is leaking. John, can you look at that?
B: Sure, no problem. I'll fix it this afternoon, OK?
A: Yes, that's fine, thanks. Secondly, one of the steps is broken. It needs welding. Sandra?
C: OK. I'll do that right away. It should take me an hour, tops.
A: Good. Can you look at the jack as well, please? It looks like it needs some grease. It's a two-minute job.
C: Sure.
A: Next, the electrics. Some of the wiring is damaged, so there are no lights. And I don't think the air conditioning is working either. I'll ask the HVAC people to have a look at those. Leave that with me. And finally, the door. The lock is broken and needs replacing. And one of the hinges needs replacing, too. John, can you do those after the roof?
B: Just to clarify – is it just the lock that needs replacing or the handle and key plate as well?
A: Just the lock. There's a broken key in it. It's a mortise lock.
B: OK, no problem.
A: Great. Thanks, everyone. Any more questions …?

▶ 💿 12

1   I can't get the genny to start. The engine is turning over, so the battery must be all right.
2   There's a problem with the JCB. The temperature gauge is showing red.
3   Listen to the bulldozer. The engine is misfiring. Any ideas what it could be?
4   Have you seen the mechanic? The gauge is showing low pressure, but the oil reservoir is full.
5   Can you look at the crane, please? It's completely dead. There are no lights, nothing.

Unit 4 Materials

▶ 🔊 13

There are basically two types of driveway. You can have a firm surface, like stones or concrete or asphalt, and you can have a loose surface of aggregate, like gravel or crushed stone. Each type needs layers of different materials underneath the surface layer, and the materials you use for these layers have different properties. So, for example, if you want paving stones, you need a bedding layer underneath, which is normally coarse sand or grit. If the sand is too fine, the bedding layer will be too soft. Under that you may have a base layer, and underneath that you may have another layer, called a sub-base. This sub-base needs to be strong enough to take the weight of vehicles, like family cars. If this sub-base is too weak, the driveway will subside, or sink. These two layers will be aggregates of different sizes. The larger aggregates are at the bottom. The sub-base sits on the sub-grade, in other words on the existing ground. On the outside you have edgings. The edgings are often stone or concrete. Some edgings, like in children's playgrounds, can be elastic. On driveways, the edgings need to be strong enough to hold the paving together. And they need to be tough. Brittle edgings are no good – they break or chip easily. Edgings also need to look attractive. So it's important to think about things like colour and finish, otherwise the finished driveway may look unattractive. You also need to take texture into account. Will the texture be rough or smooth? And then you could also …

▶ 🔊 14

When you put down asphalt, you have to think about its properties. The first is the pen value, or penetration value, which tells you how hard or soft the asphalt is. The pen value depends on the climate and the local temperatures. If the asphalt is too hard, it will crack. If it's too soft, it will distort, or change shape. The second property is cutback, which has to do with how fast the asphalt cures, in other words, how quickly it reaches maximum strength and hardness. Again, this will change depending on local conditions. Another property is porosity, or how much water the asphalt lets through. And then there's noise reduction and reflection. Both of these are important on motorways, but not so important on driveways. Motorways need to be as quiet as possible, particularly in built-up areas. And they mustn't produce glare which can affect a driver's eyes. The dark surface of the asphalt absorbs light and reduces reflection. With an asphalt surface you don't have a bedding layer, but you do have a binding layer, which holds everything together.

▶ 🔊 15

1

[A = Site Manager, of Harrogate Solutions
B = Abdulla, of Kawasoki Construction]

A: Harrogate Solutions. How can I help you?
B: Hi. My name is Abdulla. I'm calling about an order. There are a few problems with it.
A: Do you have the order number?
B: Yes, yes of course. It's J2356-G.
A: Just one moment, please. Can I just confirm your company name, please?
B: Yes, it's Kawasoki Construction.
A: Thank you. Yes, three packages of electrical supplies. It seems that the packages were dispatched at nine this morning. Just one moment. I'll call up the delivery note. Yes, it was signed for by a Mr Malik Zahid. At 10:05.
B: Malik Zahid? We don't have anyone of that name on our site. What was the delivery address?
A: 34 Bridge Street.
B: Ah, that's the problem. That's not our site. That's a couple of blocks down. It's the same street but we're at number 12.
A: Oh, I'm sorry about that. I'll sort out a new delivery straight away. It should be with you tomorrow.
B: Wait … there's no need. I'll send someone down to see Mr Zahid. It'll be quicker. I'll call again if I have any problems …

2

[A = Lopez   B = Christina Dudek]

A: Hello?
B: Just one moment, please. Sorry about that. OK, go ahead.
A: Ah, good. Thank you. My name's Lopez. Who am I speaking to, please?
B: Christina Dudek. How can I help you?
A: I'm calling about a problem with an order. We ordered some sand.
B: Hasn't it arrived?
A: Yes, yes, it's here. That's not the problem.
B: Is it the wrong sand?
A: No, it's the right sand. But it's the wrong quantity.
B: What do you mean?
A: Well, we ordered three 10 kg bags. And we received three truckloads.
B: So are you saying that we sent you three truckloads?
A: Yes, that's right. No, wait … now we have six truckloads! Three more have just arrived …
B: Where is the sand now?
A: In our car park. Our security guard didn't check the delivery – he just signed for it.
B: Oh, no.

A: Oh, yes. They unloaded six trucks before we could stop them.

B: Did you say *unloaded*? Oh, no …

3

[A = Site Manager
B = Alano Baldamero of Sevant Contractors]

A: Hello.

B: Good morning. This is Alano Baldamero from Sevant Contractors.

A: Could you repeat that, please? I didn't catch that.

B: This is Alano Baldamero from Sevant Contractors.

A: Ah, yes. Are you calling about the beams?

B: Yes, exactly. Where are they? We're waiting for them.

A: Yes, well, the driver just called. He's stuck.

B: Sorry? What do you mean?

A: He's stuck in the mud. And he can't move, he says.

B: OK. Where is he? I'll send someone to pull him out.

A: He's just off the B391, about 100 metres down the track to your site. He said he pulled over to let a wide load go past and then he got stuck.

B: Yes, I think I know the spot. We had another delivery stuck there this morning. Can you tell him we'll be there in about half an hour?

A: Yes, thank you. And one more thing …

B: Yes?

A: Any chance you could do something about the track? We'll be sending you more materials tomorrow.

B: Well, it's the rain, but I take your point. I'll see what I can do.

A: Thanks.

Unit 5 Processes

▶ 🎧 16

Setting out is basically the process of putting what was on the plan on to the ground. We use various tools and techniques to do this, ranging from simple pegs and ranging poles to sophisticated electronic equipment, depending on the job. It's all about maths. The simplest thing to set out is a straight line. As an example, let's imagine we are setting out a straight line for a new road. Let me explain the process step by step. First, we make sure we have the plans and drawings we need. Next we get the equipment. The simplest way to set out a straight line is to use three ranging poles and three plumb lines. You also need two people, an observer and an assistant. Let's say that the straight line is to go from Point A to Point B. The observer and his assistant place the ranging poles at points A and B.

It's important to use the plumb lines to make sure that the rods are vertical. Next the observer stands at Point A. The assistant places a third pole at Point C, closer to A than to B, and moves it until the observer is satisfied that it is in the correct place. Finally, the line is marked with a series of pegs, say ten metres apart. For longer distances more rods can be used.

▶ 🎧 17

[A = Susanne Kohl   B = Peter]

A: HR. Susanne Kohl speaking.

B: Hi, Susanne. It's Peter. How's it going?

A: Fine, thanks. Busy as ever.

B: You left me a message to call you …

A: Ah, yes. Have you heard the news about Sally?

B: What news?

A: She's pregnant.

B: So?

A: So you'll need a new structural engineer for your team.

B: Ah, yes, of course. When is she planning to leave?

A: She said mid-July.

B: OK. Is she coming back after she has the baby?

A: She'll decide later on. But she may take a couple of years off.

B: We'd better think about finding a replacement then. We can't cover for that long.

A: Yes. And even if she does come back, we need extra people in the team, anyway. There's a lot to do.

B: OK, so what's the procedure?

A: Well, first of all you need to identify the key skills you want her replacement to have. And then we need to prepare, or probably just update, the job description.

B: OK, that's easy enough.

A: Then we need to advertise, first internally, then externally.

B: OK.

A: Then it's a matter of looking at people's CVs, producing a shortlist and carrying out the interviews.

B: That's it?

A: Well, we'll also need to check references before we make our final decision. And then we inform the successful applicant and organise the induction.

B: OK. Look. Why don't we meet next Monday to talk about the key skills you mentioned?

A: Just a second. Let me check my diary. Yes, OK, that sounds good. Three o'clock?

B: Perfect. See you then.

18

This is what we used to do. Every day we got hundreds of invoices from different suppliers. These went straight to the accounts department. Let's imagine that the invoice was for some materials, say, a load of sand. The first thing they did was match the invoice with the purchase order (to check that we had ordered the sand) and the delivery note (to check that the sand had been received). If the documents did not match, the invoice was sent back to the supplier. If they did match, the accounts department sent the invoice, together with the purchase order and the delivery note, to the project manager for approval. Once the invoice was approved, the accounts department entered the details into the books and filed the invoices in the accounts payable file. The payment was then dealt with, normally by bank transfer, within 30 days of receipt of the invoice. The invoices then went into the paid invoices file. These files were kept for ten years.

19

That's the way we used to do it. Nowadays the system is all on computer. When the invoice comes in, it goes to the accounts department, as before. They type the process order number into the system and scan in the invoice. They also type in the date of the payment, the invoice number and the amount to be paid. The system then checks whether or not the invoice is for the right amount and if it has been approved. If everything is OK, the authorisation is given for payment to be made. It's much easier, much faster and there are fewer mistakes.

Unit 6 Projects

20

Welcome to this kick-off meeting. I just want to clarify some points about how I see this project running. First of all, I want to stress the importance of the project plan, which is this document, and which covers all aspects of the project. Among other things, it outlines the scope, in other words the work that needs to be done in order for the project to be completed successfully. All of us need to be very familiar with this document. In fact, by the end of next week, I expect us all to know this document better than our own partners. The second document is the WBS, or Work Breakdown Structure. This splits the work into smaller elements which are easier to manage in terms of resources, costs, and so on. Each of you will be responsible for your own elements in the WBS, but it's important that you see the big picture, too.

21

As I see it, I'm really concerned with three issues: *cost*, in other words keeping to budget; *time*, or keeping to the schedule and meeting our deadlines; and *scope*, which is, as I explained earlier, the work that needs to be done. A change in one of these issues affects the other two. Don't get me wrong, I know changes will happen: change is part of any project. My main job is to continually monitor what's happening, so that I know where we are in terms of the project plan and so that I can fix any problems.

22

1   <u>We</u> need to get the roof finished before the rainy season starts.
2   We need to get the <u>roof</u> finished before the rainy season starts.
3   We need to get the roof finished <u>before</u> the rainy season starts.
4   We need to get the roof <u>finished</u> before the rainy season starts.
5   We need to get the roof finished before the <u>rainy</u> season starts.

Thank you all for coming at such short notice. What I want to talk about is *communication*. Things are not going well. I know that we're all very busy, and that we're all members of other project teams. I also understand that we all come from different companies and have different ways of working. But we need to improve our communication, otherwise we are never going to meet all our deadlines and finish this project on time.

I've discussed the communication problem with the directors, and we feel there are a number of things we can do to solve the problem. First of all, we need to have more meetings – face-to-face or at least online. Secondly, we all use the intranet already, so we have decided to set up a new portal, which will include project updates, documentation, Gantt charts – that is to say project schedules – and tools and templates. There will also be information about team members, specialists, previous experience and so on. We basically need to get to know each other better. And finally, the HR department has contacted a company who will organise team-building activities for us, which I will tell you about later. Again, this will help us work better as a team.

[A = Client   B = Consultant]

A: What about types of contracts?

B: There are many different types of contracts.

A: What do you mean?

B: Well, let's take the simplest contract – a lump sum contract. In this contract the client agrees to pay a fixed amount of money for the finished product.

A: I see. So the client knows exactly how much the project will cost?

B: Yes, exactly. But if there are any problems, the contractor has to pay the extra costs. The contractor is taking the risk.

A: I see. So it's good for the client?

B: Not always. A contractor might use cheap materials to lower the costs.

A: Ah, OK. What other types are there?

B: Another type is a cost plus contract. This means that the client pays all the costs of the project, plus extra payment so that the contractor makes a profit.

A: I see. And how is the extra payment calculated?

B: There are different ways. For example, in a cost plus fixed fee contract the client covers all the costs, including any cost overruns, but the contractor only gets a fixed fee, so there is an incentive to finish the job quickly.

A: OK.

B: You could also have a cost plus fixed fee plus a bonus for work that is finished ahead of time. Or a bonus for any savings that the contractor makes. And so on.

A: Yes, yes, of course.

B: And then there are turnkey projects.

A: Turnkey?

B: Turnkey means that one person, or company, is responsible for all the work. Normally a client has to work with a designer such as an architect and a contractor, who is responsible for the building. In a turnkey solution, the client only has to speak to one person who is responsible for the whole project and at the end gives the key to the client. Nice and simple ...

Unit 7 Documentation

[A = Manager   B = New employee
C = Jeff, a document controller]

A: This room is, in a way, the heart of the company. Everything comes into or goes out from here.

B: What do you mean?

A: Well, our company deals with hundreds of documents relating to all the different projects, you know, documents such as correspondence, job site memos, change orders, reports, drawings, RFI logs, procedures and so on. So document control is very important. All documents come through this room. These people – the document controllers – are responsible for looking after the documents so that they are in the right place at the right time or can be accessed whenever they are needed. Any delays cost money.

B: I see. Erm ... you said RFI logs?

A: Oh, yes. RFI stands for 'request for information'. It's a document that asks for information about specific details in a project. And an RFI *log* is a *list* of the RFIs.

B: Ah, yes, of course. But ... isn't it all done on computer?

A: Well, yes and no. Yes, we do use computers, of course. But no, because we still get a lot of documentation which isn't in electronic format, so that has to be processed manually. Of course we scan a lot of documentation, but that takes time – logging it in, giving it a serial number, tracking it so that we know where it is, making sure it gets booked out to the right person, making copies or backups, that sort of thing.

B: I see.

A: But I think we'll have to change to a better system soon. It's not only processing this volume of documents that takes time, but also managing all the amendments. There are always draft versions of documents which need to be replaced or updated. If we had a fully integrated system, I'm sure things would be faster and more efficient.

B: What's in that room over there?

A: Those are the archives. We have to keep certain documents for up to three years, according to the law. We also keep confidential documents in there, in a safe.

[A = office worker B = employee]

A: First you have to type in a password. OK, good, so this is a typical document. You can see the first button on the top left says Details. That's the document serial number and document type – a drawing, a memo, an agenda or whatever. And the next button is the Status. If you click on Status, you get two options – draft or final.

B: Yes. OK.

A: And next to it is the Confidentiality level button. We have three levels: *restricted* documents can only be seen by certain people, *internal* documents are for our use only and *open* documents, which anyone can see.

B: Uh-huh, all right.

A: Moving across, you can see the Originator button, which is normally someone's name – but it could also be a department – and their contact telephone number and email address. Then there's the Document history button, which is a list of the different versions of the documents, together with dates and the people involved.

B: OK.

A: And if you click this button, you get the Document output menu. We can set different possibilities, for example, 'only allow online viewing', or 'transfer files', or 'print'. And for special documents, like big drawings, we can click here and that sends the drawings straight to the printer.

B: I see.

27

[A = Thomas   B = Vince]

A: Hi Vince. It's Thomas.

B: Thomas. What's up?

A: I just received some changes to some of the drawings. I thought I'd phone and tell you.

B: Can't you just send them?

A: Yes, but they wouldn't get to you before this afternoon. And you're already working on the foundations, aren't you?

B: The foundations? They want changes to the foundations?

A: Only minor amendments, don't worry.

B: I hope so. OK. I'll just get the drawings. Which ones do I need?

A: The drawing number is GF/400/013. Well, it says 013, but it should be 003. Foundations – warehouse, the third row on the schedule of drawings. You need the general notes for that.

B: OK. Hang on a second. OK, got them. 003, not 013. OK. What are the other changes?

A: You see note 2, load bearing walls? The specs have been modified.

B: Note 2. Load bearing walls. Got it.

A: It should read 250 mm thick, not 200.

B: OK. 250, not 200. Anything else?

A: Yes. Note 3, Roman numeral 2. They think that the blinding ratios should be 1 to 3 to 6, not to 5.

B: OK, 1 to 3 to 6. And they call these minor changes, huh?

A: The next one is minor. Very minor. You see the abbreviation in note 6? There's a typo.

B: Yeah, yeah. It should read BS, not GS. No problem. Anything else?

A: The semi-colon at the end of note 6 should be a full stop.

B: Yes, yes, OK.

A: And you see the plumbing? Bottom right-hand corner?

B: Yes.

A: There's nothing wrong with it. You'll get the revised drawings this afternoon.

B: OK. Thanks, Thomas. And it's a good thing you called. We were just starting to mix the cement.

A: I saved you a bit of time, then.

B: Yes. Right, gotta go. I need to sort this out asap.

28

[A = Alexandra Puccini, Ministry of Public Works
B = Mustafa Mohammed Al Najashi
C = Hamish Campbell, head of department at Ministry of Public Works]

A: Ministry of Public Works. Alexandra Puccini speaking.

B: Hello? Is that the Ministry of Public Works?

A: Yes, that's right. How can I help you?

B: I'd like to speak to somebody about a tender we'd like to submit.

A: One moment, please. I'll put you through to Hamish Campbell.

B: Thank you.

C: Hello. Hamish Campbell speaking.

B: Hello, Mr Kandell. My name is Mustafa Mohammed Al Najashi. I'd like to speak to someone about a tender.

C: The name's Campbell, not Kandell.

B: Oh, I'm sorry, Mr Campbell.

C: No problem. A tender? Do you have a project number?

B: Yes, it's KZH 897.

C: KZH 897? One moment, please. Ah, yes. It's to do with the tunnel refurbishment on Highway 36.

B: Yes, that's right.

C: How can I help you?

B: It's about an email which I sent you on the 27th of May, confirming that my company would like to bid for the project and asking for more information. But I haven't received anything. And I believe the submission date is next week.

C: What did you say your name was?

B: Mustafa Mohammed Al Najashi.

C: Ah, yes, yes. Mr Al Najashi. Is it your company which is doing the bridge refurbishment on the same highway?

B: Yes, that's right.

C: Yes, yes, I remember. Ah, I've found it now. We sent you a reply asking for your postal address, but I'm afraid the email bounced.

B: Bounced?

C: Yes. The address is unknown.

B: Ah, wait a minute. What email address did you send it to?

C: mman@psl.net.

B: Ah, no, no. That email address is no good. It's been changed. I'm sorry. My new address is mman@psl.com.

C: I see. No problem. You're still in time if you'd like to submit a tender.

B: Thank you. Will you send me the necessary information?

C: Yes, but I do need your postal address first. I'd like to send you the information pack, but it's not available in digital format. Snail mail, I'm afraid.

B: Of course. It's … erm … are you ready?

Unit 8 Health and safety

▶ 💿 29

So, to recap, here are the five most important things I have covered in today's talk. First of all, hazardous waste. Waste needs to be sorted properly and dealt with properly. Just follow the instructions and take proper precautions. Next, falls, which is one of the most common causes of accidents. People fall off scaffolding, off ladders, off roofs. Don't climb on things which aren't fixed properly. And don't cut corners. Take your time. Don't forget, height can kill. Third, cranes and loads, which are just as dangerous. People either fall off things or things fall on them. Keep your eyes open. And remember, don't rig loads unless you are trained to do it. Next, watch out when trucks are loading or unloading. As I said, last year three people on sites near here died by being buried alive. One of them was buried in sand just like this. And finally, PPE: Personal Protective Equipment. We give you this equipment because it helps to keep you safe. Remember: use the equipment. Wear your hard hat. Follow the recommendations. Any questions?

▶ 💿 30

Right, listen up. Here's what's going to happen. We're going to park the vehicle just in front of the work area, to give us protection from oncoming traffic. Bob, I want you and Ali to put out the signs. Put out the 'keep right' signs first, and then the 'road narrows' signs, and lastly the 'road works' signs. Make sure the 'road works' sign is at least 50 metres away from the end of the taper. That's the wide end, not the narrow end. Do our side of the road first and then the other side, OK? Good. The rest of you will put out the cones. I'll stay in the middle and do the barrier. We need at least 5 metres between the cones, and the taper needs to be around 25 metres long. Start from the kerb and face the traffic as you work. The volume of traffic here isn't very high, but it's better to be safe. And don't forget to keep the safety zone clear. Any questions about that?

▶ 💿 31

1 A: A friend of mine had white finger syndrome from using vibrating power tools. He lost all feeling in his hands.

  B: Sounds painful.

2 A: I had an accident last year. I tripped over a cable and fell. I put out my arm to stop myself and broke my wrist.

  B: Ouch. I bet that hurt.

3 A: I saw an accident this morning. One of the labourers dropped a load of bricks on his foot. He was only wearing sandals, not safety boots, which didn't help.

  B: What? I'll speak to the manager. Everyone needs boots.

4 A: Back injuries are very common. People lift things which are too heavy.

  B: Straight back, bend the knees. That's what I always say.

5 A: One of the drivers was hit by a truck. He wasn't wearing his hi-vis vest and the other driver didn't see him. The bumper hit his leg just below his knee and fractured it.

  B: I bet he wears his vest from now on.

6 A: People don't use ear protection and then damage their hearing. It's a gradual process, so they're not aware of what's happening.

  B: Pardon? What did you say?

Pearson Education Limited
Edinburgh Gate
Harlow
Essex CM20 2JE
England
and Associated Companies throughout the world.

www.pearsonelt.com

© Pearson Education Limited 2012

The right of Evan Frendo to be identified as author of this
Work has been asserted by him in accordance with the
Copyright, Designs and Patents Act 1988.

First published 2012

ISBN: 978-1-4082-6992-3

Set in ITC Cheltenham Book
Printed by Graficas Estella, Spain

Acknowledgements
The publishers and author would like to thank the following
people for their feedback and comments during the
development of the material:

Julie Cordell-Szczurek, Germany; Edward Halton, UAE;
Pamela Heath, Canada; Teresa and Tony Higgins, UK;
Sotirios Koutskoukos, UK

We are grateful to the following for permission to reproduce
copyright material:

Figures
Figure on page 9 after Europass CV template, http://
europass.cedefop.europa.eu/img/dynamic/c1344/type.
FileContent.file/CVTemplate_en_GB.doc, © European
Union, 2004-2010, http://europass.cedefop.europa.eu.

Logos
Logo on page 16 FSC® logo 'The Mark of Responsible
Forestry' is reproduced with permission from Forest
Stewardship Council.

Text
Extract on p.10 from IFC Seoul Financial Center, posted
by Wendy Cohn, http://blog.zumllc.com/?p=52, with
permission from Zumllc; Extract on page 10 from Top
steel firms by Alison Luke, 13th June 2009, http://www.
constructionweekonline.com/article-5517-top-steel-firms/1/
print/, copyright Construction Week; Extract on page 10
from Otis Wins Contract For Landmark Development in
Seoul, News release, Otis Elevator Company, http://www.
prnewswire.com/news-releases/otis-wins-contract-for-
landmark-development-in-seoul-64920832.html, courtesy
of Otis Elevator Company; Extract on page 34 adapted
from Architectural, construction and environmental matters
of Bahrain's International Formula 1 Circuit, Building
and Environment, 42 (4), pp.1785-1786 (Alnaser, N. W.,
Flanagan, R., Al-Khalifa, S. E., Mumtaz, R., El-Masri, S.,
Alnaser, W. E. 2007), Copyright 2007, with permission from
Elsevier; Extract on page 58 from The Castle Golf Design
and Build Process, http://www.castlegolf.com/minigolf_
process.html, with permission from Castle Golf, Inc.

In some instances we have been unable to trace the
owners of copyright material, and we would appreciate any
information that would enable us to do so.
p.10 – Invest Korea (3 short extracts)
p.10 – Siemens (1 short extract)
p.50 – Egis Projects (Focus on a project: Wroclaw-Katowice
Motorway, Poland)
p.54 – Bulding in Canada (Plumbing Legend)
p.66 – Hurricaine preparation tips (Florida Home Builders
Association)

Photo ackowledgements
The publishers would like to thank the following for their
kind permission to reproduce their photographs:

(Key: b-bottom; c-centre; l-left; r-right; t-top)

8 Shutterstock.com: Celeborn. **10 Ottmar Bierwagen:**
Spectrum Photofile / photographersdirect.com.
18 Heliobus ® AG. 21 Fotolia.com: photosoup (tl); James
Phelps (r). **Pearson Education Ltd:** Photodisc (bc);
Gareth Boden (tc). **26 Alamy Images:** Michael Molloy
(l); Alistair Laming (br). **© Cantideck, image used with
permission:** (tc). **KONE plc:** (tr). **Photograph courtesy
of Byrne Bros:** (bc). **27 Shutterstock.com:** Neil Balderson.
28 Shutterstock.com: hfng. **31 Pearson Education Ltd:**
Image Source (l). **Shutterstock.com:** appalachian trail (r).
34 Reuters: Stringer. **42 Reuters:** Jo Yong hak (b). **Rex
Features:** Sipa Press (t). **58 Courtesy of Adventure Golf,
www.adventuregolf.com. 66 DK Images:** Chris Orr (tr).
Rex Features: Action Press (l)

Cover images: *Front:* **Alamy Images:** Paul Bradbury c,
Peter Alvey r; **Corbis:** Alan Schein Photography
background; **SuperStock:** age fotostock l

Every effort has been made to trace the copyright holders
and we apologise in advance for any unintentional
omissions. We would be pleased to insert the appropriate
acknowledgement in any subsequent edition of this
publication.